HEARING GOD'S VOICE

I0157373

FACILITATOR MANUAL

ZⱰE

Some study note quotes taken from the Holy Bible, New International Version ®. NIV ®. Copyright © 1973, 1978, 1984, 2011 by Biblica, Inc. ®. Used by permission of Zondervan. All rights reserved worldwide. www.zondervan.com

Quotes used by permission from Finis Jennings Dake, Sr., Author of *Dake's Annotated Reference Bible.*

Some quotes taken from *Ryrie Study Bible (NAS)* by Charles Caldwell Ryrie, Th.D. Copyright © 1978, Moody Bible Institute of Chicago, Moody Press. Used by permission.

Some quotes are from *Thayer's Greek-English Lexicon of the New Testament* by Joseph H. Thayer, Copyright © by Hendrickson Publishers, Peabody, Massachusetts. Used by permission. All rights reserved.

Some quotes are taken from *The Eerdman's Bible Dictionary.* Copyright © 1987 Used by permission William B Eerdmans Publishing Company. All rights reserved.

Rev. 10/22

ACKNOWLEDGMENTS

ZOE Ministries International is dedicated to training, equipping and sending believers into the world to minister by the leading of the Holy Spirit. This ministry helps build the body of Christ and encourages God's people to use their gifts and talents for His glory. It is for this purpose that this manual has been compiled by the leading of the Holy Spirit and the input of many people. ZOE Ministries wishes to thank them for their support, time, and talents in putting this manual together. We give our Lord all the praise and glory for this work!

CONTENTS

This material is designed to be used within a specific format.
Facilitator Training is a necessary prerequisite before this material
may be used effectively in a Bible study or class setting.

We praise the Lord that He has led you to become involved with ZOE Ministries as you prepare to lead or assist in this **Hearing God's Voice** course. It is with joy that we tell you that through this course and the other **"Hearing, Knowing and Following God's Voice"** courses, lives are being radically changed for the Lord! We truly believe that as you facilitate this course and allow the Holy Spirit the freedom He needs and deserves, you will see God move in miraculous ways.

This curriculum has been developed under the Lord's leading by many individuals and refined and revised through many class presentations over the past several years. We believe the format and order of presentation are important and urge you to follow the course outline and the **Facilitator Manual.**

The Word says, **"My sheep hear My voice, and I know them, and they follow Me" John 10:27 (NKJ).** Take this scripture and apply it in the course and watch the Lord work! To God be the glory!

May God bless you and your group as you learn to listen to God's voice.

In Christ,

Dick and Ginny Chanda
Founders/Directors

INTRODUCTORY COMMENTS
TO FACILITATORS

As an introduction to this manual, we have summarized information that we feel will be helpful to you during this course. Much of this information was covered during your facilitator training.

- DIRECTIONAL INFORMATION FOR FACILITATORS IS OUTLINED IN THIS FONT FOR QUICK IDENTIFICATION.

- Remember, do not just teach this material unless you are instructed to do so in the manual. As a facilitator, you need to remember that you are a coach and you are there to encourage class participation.

- Please don't read the Supporting Principles From Scripture sections until you have prayerfully studied the assigned passages first. Allow God to work in your life through His Word, and then read the Manual to help you see the connection between the Scriptures and the main principle of each lesson.

- The first few lessons of this course will have a more instructional format. Some of the early lessons include teachings that provide a common base of understanding for your class members.

- In this **Hearing God's Voice** course, the facilitator will lead all discussions through Lesson 4. In Lesson 5 the facilitator will lead the Scripture discussion, and a participant will be asked to lead the book discussion. In Lessons 6-11, participants will be asked to lead all the discussions. The facilitator will lead the discussion in Lesson 12.

- If a lesson contains a teaching, please let the class know that you are teaching from the Facilitator Manual provided by ZOE Ministries International.

- Lessons without teachings provide you with an opportunity to model how participants should lead class discussions later in the course.

- As a facilitator, it is your responsibility to encourage the class to share the insights that God gave them as they studied the assigned material. Ask questions that will draw out these insights.

- You are not expected, nor should you attempt, to cover every point in each lesson. These points are provided for your edification and only those that directly support the main principle should be included in the class discussion.

- As participants become more involved in leading class discussions, your primary purpose is to coordinate the class and allow the Lord to build individuals' confidence and leadership abilities.

- Look for participants who, with practice, would make good facilitators. After the course, suggest that they go through Facilitator Training.

- If during a class discussion someone's answer or insight is "not quite right," please do not directly address this with the individual. Instead, redirect the discussion back to the main principle of the lesson.

- Remember, as a facilitator, you cannot solve each person's problems. You are to present principles from God's Word and allow the Holy Spirit to help class members apply them to their lives.

- Finally, we respectfully ask that this copyrighted material not be copied or reproduced for other purposes without express written permission of ZOE Ministries International.

We request this not to "control" the material, but for two reasons:

1) Without proper facilitator training, the course will not be what we feel the Holy Spirit wants it to be, and

2) We need to honor those who have graciously given us permission to reprint or quote their materials. As stewards of their authorship, we are responsible for not using this material beyond the limitations that they have requested.

Thank you for your involvement in this **Hearing Gods Voice** course and we join you in praying that the Holy Spirit will transform participants' lives!

LESSON 1

INTRODUCTION

MAIN PRINCIPLE

God wants all of His children to be disciples of Jesus and to hear, know and follow His voice. We can hear God's specific word for us in every area of our lives.

LESSON 1

Introduction

NOTE TO THE FACILITATOR:

YOU WILL BE FACILITATING LESSONS 1–4. BE PREPARED TO COVER THE MATERIAL IN THE BOOK, SCRIPTURE AND ARTICLES. LESSONS 1, 2 AND 4 REQUIRE MORE TEACHING THAN CLASS DISCUSSION. LESSONS 1 AND 2 ARE DESIGNED TO GIVE AN OVERVIEW OF WHAT IS INVOLVED IN HEARING GOD'S VOICE. LESSONS 3 AND 5 WILL PROVIDE AN OPPORTUNITY TO MODEL FOR THE CLASS HOW TO FACILITATE FUTURE CLASS DISCUSSIONS.

I. Let's Get Started!

A. WELCOME THE CLASS AND INTRODUCE YOURSELF.

B. OPEN WITH PRAYER.

C. GET ACQUAINTED WITH ONE ANOTHER. ASK EVERYONE TO BRIEFLY SHARE SOMETHING ABOUT THEMSELVES, E.G., WHETHER THEY ARE MARRIED, HAVE CHILDREN, ETC. BEGIN BY SHARING ABOUT YOURSELF.

D. DIRECT THE CLASS TO THE ARTICLE **"A NOTE TO COURSE PARTICIPANTS"** ON PAGE 9 OF THE STUDY GUIDE. HAVE PARTICIPANTS READ PORTIONS ALOUD.

E. WORSHIP THE LORD.
(DECIDE WHETHER YOUR CLASS SHOULD
TAKE TIME TO WORSHIP DURING THIS
LESSON.) SHARE THE FOLLOWING WITH THE
CLASS, AS THE LORD LEADS:

There are several reasons why we take class time to
worship. Besides the fact that He is worthy of our praise,
worship prepares our hearts to better hear God during
class. It helps us get our eyes off ourselves and back on
the Lord. Worship reminds us of God's love, faithfulness
and awesome power.

II. Introduction to ZOE Ministries International

A. The Purpose of ZOE Ministries

Zoe is a Greek word for *life* found in many Scriptures,
including **John 17:3. "Now this is eternal life: that they
may know you, the only true God, and Jesus Christ,
whom you have sent."** The purpose of ZOE Ministries
is to bring forth *zoe*, God's vibrant life, in individual
believers so that their daily lives glorify God as they
minister that life to others.

B. The Goal of ZOE Ministries

1. Our goal is to train and equip believers to
   make disciples, which is in keeping with the
   commission given to us by Jesus in **Matthew
   28:19–20—"Therefore go and make disciples of
   all nations, baptizing them in the name of the
   Father and of the Son and of the Holy Spirit,
   and teaching them to obey everything I have**

commanded you. And surely I am with you
always, to the very end of the age."

2. How do we accomplish our goal of making disciples?

a. **By training and equipping through our courses**

- **Hearing, Knowing and Following God's Voice**
  — This series of 12-week discipleship courses
  can help us hear God's voice in various aspects
  of Christian life. They provide discipleship in a
  group setting.

- **Discipleship by the Word of God and the
  Power of the Holy Spirit**—This course provides
  training on how to disciple individuals one-on-
  one, thereby allowing them to take great strides in
  their personal relationship with God and ministry.
  This method of discipleship uses the Word and
  the leading of the Holy Spirit as the only tools.
  It is changing lives in a very simple, yet powerful
  way.

- **Captivated by Their Character**—To meet the
  need for evangelistic outreach, we have designed
  a home-based series of lessons. This three-part
  series is designed for the unbeliever, new believer,
  or those who need a refresher on the Trinity.
  The six-week courses are:
  1. Who Is Jesus?
  2. Who Is the Father?
  3. Who Is the Holy Spirit?

b. **By imparting God's life**
  Our mission is to impart God's life *(zoe)* into the hearts
  of responsive people. We desire to see that *zoe* life

manifested in individual believers, so that their daily lives glorify God as they minister that life to others.

c. **By connecting the Bride of Christ (the Church) with the Bridegroom**
Our heart is to see a holy, Spirit-led bride become alive with a burning passion for our soon-coming King, Judge and Bridegroom. God has called us to do this by training the bride (the Church) to **hear, know** and **follow** God's voice.

3. In making disciples, we often focus on evangelism—helping people come to a saving knowledge of Jesus. However, Billy Graham has said that 5% of the effort in disciple-making is winning the soul, while 95% is discipleship. What exactly is a disciple?

"A *disciple* is one who follows the disciple-maker's teaching and becomes attached to his teacher."[1] In **John 8:31,** Jesus described what a disciple of His is like: **"If you abide in My word [hold fast to my teachings and live in accordance with them], you are truly My disciples" (AMP).**

4. We are called to help make *disciples of Jesus*—believers who know and love Jesus, and who follow Jesus in doctrine and conduct of life.

a. Jesus said in **Luke 6:40, "A student is not above his teacher, but everyone who is fully trained will be like his teacher."**

b. Jesus was a good disciple of God the Father. He said in **John 14:31, "But the world must learn that I love the Father and that I do exactly what** my **Father has commanded me."** See also **John 5:19** and **John 8:28.**

  c. A disciple of Jesus can also be defined as one who:
  - loves Jesus deeply and is captivated by Him
  - loves others with His love
  - learns to do the works of Jesus

  d. **Luke 9** and **10** tell of Jesus first sending out His 12 disciples and then 70 (or 72) others. They went out and did the works of Jesus; they preached that the kingdom of God is at hand, they healed the sick, and delivered those who were oppressed by evil spirits.

We see Jesus' response at His disciples' return in **Luke 10:21, "At that time Jesus, full of joy through the Holy Spirit, said, 'I praise you, Father, Lord of heaven and earth, because you have hidden these things from the wise and learned, and revealed them to little children. Yes, Father, for this was your good pleasure.'"**

Jesus was **"full of joy."** This phrase in the Greek indicates that He was exuberant—He literally jumped up and down.[2] Jesus was ecstatic! Jesus takes that much delight in *our* obeying His Word and following His example.

III. Scriptural Principles for "How to Hear God's Voice"

READ, OR HAVE SOMEONE READ, THE MAIN PRINCIPLE FOR TODAY'S LESSON.

From **Genesis** to **Revelation** the Word expresses God's desire to speak to His children! The following story illustrates God's desire to speak to us.

A. Share the following true story by Steve Lightle from his book, Exodus II—Let My People Go.

I had read the verses in **John 10** where four times Jesus said, **"My sheep know My voice." John 18:37** says, **"... Every one who is of the truth hears My voice."** When I read these, I said, "Wow! I know You Jesus. I'm born of the truth. But, I need to hear Your voice, Lord!" And so I said, "Oh, Lord, I want to hear Your voice! I want to hear Your voice! Speak to me!"

Even though He had spoken to me on several other occasions, it was something that seemed so rare. I wanted to have daily fellowship and communion with Jesus so that I could hear His voice regularly.

Then one night—a cold night in February—Judy and I were sleeping as usual with the windows open. There was snow on the ground and it seemed almost colder inside the room than outside. At about 2:30 a.m., all of a sudden I was wide awake. This was very unusual for me. Normally, I can sleep through anything. I thought, "What in the world am I doing awake?" Then it dawned on me that maybe it was the Lord's doing.

"Lord, did You wake me up?"

And that still inner voice spoke to me and said, "Yes, son."

That response was really something. I remember how there was such a settling of security in my heart when the Lord said "son." It established who He is and who I am. He's my Father and I'm His son.

"Oh, Lord, what do You want?" I said.

And the Lord spoke in a very clear voice in my heart and He said, "I want you to get out of bed. I want you to lie on the floor because I have something I want to tell you."

"Lord," I said, "I'll just lie right here in my nice warm bed and You can tell me what You want to tell me. It would be cold if I got out and laid on the floor."

"No," the Lord said. "I told you to get up, get out of bed, and lie down on the floor because I have something to tell you."

"Lord, no," I argued. "Tell me why. I want to stay here in this warm bed." This exchange went on several times.

The Lord got rather stern with me in His voice. Finally I said, "Okay, I'll do it." And so I got up out of bed and it was cold! The Lord had told me to lie at the foot of the bed, which was hardwood flooring. And I thought, "Oh, this is really going to be cold!" And when I went there and laid down, God had supernaturally heated the spot on the floor. It was as though I was lying on a beach in Hawaii. I was so thrilled!

If I hadn't been obedient and gotten up out of that bed, I would have missed that experience.

I began to worship and praise the Lord. I lost track of time. Then I remembered. "Lord, You wanted to tell me something. What is it You wanted to tell me?"

"I wanted to tell you that you could get up and go back to bed."

"What?" I was shocked.

"Yes, you can get up and get into bed."

"I don't understand," I complained. "You tell me to get out of bed. I get out. You said to lie down at the foot of the bed. I laid down here. And now You tell me the thing You wanted to tell me was that I could go back and get in bed?"

"Yes," He said. "I wanted to see if you would obey Me. It's not just good enough to hear My voice. I wanted to see if you would obey me in something small."

The Lord taught me that if I would be obedient to His voice in the little things, then He would begin to give me other more important opportunities. I didn't realize that there would be a time coming in my life when that same voice that tested me and taught me that night would be the one that would speak to me when I was ministering behind the Iron Curtain and say, "Don't go to that place," and it would save my life.[3]

//

God teaches us to hear and obey His voice in little things first.

//

B. What are the prerequisites to hearing God's voice?

Prerequisite #1—You must be born again.

John 3:3–6 says:

> In reply Jesus declared, "I tell you the truth, no one can see the kingdom of God unless he is born again."
>
> "How can a man be born when he is old?" Nicodemus asked. "Surely he cannot enter a second time into his mother's womb to be born!"
>
> Jesus answered, "I tell you the truth no one can enter the kingdom of God unless he is born of water and the Spirit. Flesh gives birth to flesh, but the Spirit gives birth to spirit."

What happens when you are born again?

Ezekiel 36:26–27 says, **"I will give you a new heart and put a new spirit in you; I will remove from you your heart of stone and give you a heart of flesh. And I will put my Spirit in you and move you to follow my decrees and be careful to keep my laws."** So, your *spirit* is born again.

Following is a recounting of a real life experience that helps illustrate what happens when you are born again. This is the story as told by one of the founders of ZOE Ministries:

I had been trying to explain to a friend about what it means to be born again. We were both frustrated at my inability to explain salvation in a way he could understand. So, I was thinking about this and was asking God, "What actually happens to us on the inside when we accept Jesus as Savior?" Then I became aware that the Lord was showing me a tall, clear, cylindrical glass about three-fourths full of white milk. I asked, "Lord, what does that mean?"
The Lord said to me, "That glass represents your body and the milk represents your spirit."

I saw a can of Hershey's chocolate syrup on the table next to the glass. (Now, I don't usually have visions of chocolate. I'm actually not fond of chocolate, so I remember thinking it was significant that there would be a can of chocolate.)

Then, I saw what appeared to be a hand pick up the can of chocolate and pour the syrup into the glass of milk. I watched as the chocolate syrup settled to the bottom of the glass. I thought, "I wonder what that represents."

The Lord said to me, "The glass represents your body, the milk represents your spirit, and the chocolate represents what happens when you are born again—My Spirit comes and lives in your spirit and you become born again."

I thought, "That's interesting, Lord. Look at how the chocolate has settled."

The Lord said, "This is what happens to people who are born again and don't do anything more in their walk with Christ."

Then I saw the hand holding a spoon. The spoon was inserted into the glass and it stirred up the chocolate milk. I became excited as I saw the chocolate and the milk become blended together. I asked, "What is happening, Lord?"

The Lord said, "The spoon represents spending time with Me in prayer, worship and My Word."

I realized that when we spend time praying, worshiping God, and reading His Word, then God's Spirit and our spirit become blended together.

Then I saw the spoon whipping up the chocolate and the milk, and the milk flowed over the glass out on to the table. When I saw the milk spilling out, I was reminded of **John 7:38, "He who believes in me, as the Scripture has said, out of his heart will flow rivers of living water" (NKJV).** I realized that as we spend time with the Lord, out of our hearts will flow rivers of living water. We should be touching people's lives with the *zoe* kind of life.

I got really excited. I thought, "Now I can go and explain this to my friend!"

But, then I felt another nudge from the Lord saying, "We're not finished yet." I watched as the spoon was taken out of the milk. I saw the chocolate settle to the bottom of the glass again.

The Lord said, "This is what happens to people who do not spend time daily with me. The glass represents their body, the milk represents their spirit, and the chocolate is my Spirit. They are born again, but without spending time with Me in the Word, worship and prayer, they can not be as effective for My kingdom."

//

God desires to fellowship with us as we spend time reading Scripture and worshiping Him and conversing with Him. He wants to fill us to overflowing with rivers of living water.

//

Prerequisite #2—You must expect to hear God.

If you have been born again, you are a child of God. Children of God can expect to be led by the Spirit and to hear God's voice. **"For as many as are led by the Spirit of God, they are the sons of God" Romans 8:14 (KJV).**

"My sheep *hear* my voice, and I *know* them, and they *follow* me" John 10:27 (KJV). Let us look at the full meaning of this verse.

a. *Hear*—translated from the Greek word *akouo* (ak-oo´-o)—to listen to, to understand, to hear with intent to obey.[4]

We, as God's sheep, should be able to hear God's voice. **"He who belongs to God hears what God says..." John 8:47.**

b. *Know*—*ginosko* (ghin-oce´-ko)—to know experientially with personal understanding; to know intimately as in a sexual relationship between male and female.[5] The best example of this knowing is the relationship God the Father has with Jesus. God knows each of us this intimately and desires that we know Him. **"He calls His own sheep by name and leads them out" John 10:3.**

c. *Follow—akoloutheo* (ak-ol-oo-theh´-o)— to cleave steadfastly to one; to conform wholly to his example in living and, if need be, in dying also.[6]

We, as God's sheep, should follow Jesus' example and His Spirit's leading. **"To obey is better than sacrifice..."** 1 Samuel 15:22.

A good maxim to remember is: It is better to follow and fail than fail to follow!

IV. Class Format — Lessons 2–12

A. Opening Time

This includes welcoming the class, prayer for that session, worshiping the Lord (unless in a shortened class), sharing what God has done in the previous week, and making announcements.

B. Discussion of the Book, Scripture and Articles

1. The reading assignments for each week are listed on the course outline in the Study Guide. MAKE SURE EVERYONE UNDERSTANDS WHAT THEY ARE SUPPOSED TO READ FOR LESSON 2 AND REVIEW THE MAIN PRINCIPLE FOR NEXT WEEK'S LESSON.

2. Everyone needs to come prepared to share what they learned, as the Lord leads.

3. The facilitator and assistant will lead the book, article and Scripture discussions through Lesson 4.

4. Beginning in Lesson 5, one participant will be asked to lead the book discussion. A facilitator will lead the Scripture discussion. In Lesson 6, one participant will be assigned to lead the Scripture discussion. Another participant will be assigned to lead the book and the assigned article discussions.

5. We cannot emphasize enough the importance of everyone asking the Holy Spirit for new insights from the Scriptures.

C. Prayer and Ministry

A prayer and ministry time will end each lesson.

D. Class Length

The length of the class is approximately 2–2½ hours (1½ hours for a shortened class).

E. Following the Holy Spirit's Guidance

We will be open to change as the Holy Spirit leads. For example, if time is a concern, He may direct us to drop the discussion of an article.

V. Your Responsibility as a Participant

REFER THE CLASS TO THE ARTICLE ABOUT THE PARTICIPANT'S RESPONSIBILITIES IN THEIR STUDY GUIDE. GO OVER THIS ARTICLE WITH THEM NOW.

In addition, class members should keep confidential everything that is shared during class.

VI. Class Article

POINT OUT TO THE CLASS THE DISCLAIMER PLACED BEFORE THE FIRST ARTICLE IN LESSON ONE OF THE STUDY GUIDE.

HAVE THE CLASS TAKE TURNS READING A PORTION OF THIS ARTICLE ALOUD. ANYONE MAY PASS IF THEY CHOOSE NOT TO READ.

VII. Ministry Time

A. AS FACILITATOR, YOU NEED TO GUIDE THE MINISTRY TIME. REFER TO THE CLASS FORMAT SECTION OF THE *FACILITATOR TRAINING STUDY GUIDE* AND READ THE "MINISTRY TIME" SECTION. (Note: The *Facilitator Training Study Guide* is the booklet you received during Facilitator Training.)

B. DURING THE MINISTRY TIME, WE SUGGEST THAT YOU DO NOT ASK CLASS MEMBERS FOR THEIR PRAYER REQUESTS. SAY TO THE PARTICIPANTS, "In general, in this course we wait until Lesson 5 to begin personal prayer ministry. In Lesson 5 we will begin praying for each lesson's discussion leaders during the ministry time."

C. ON THE OTHER HAND, IF YOU SENSE THE LORD DIRECTING YOU TO ADDRESS THE NEED FOR PERSONAL PRAYER MINISTRY IN A CLASS MEMBER, ASK THE PERSON CONCERNED IF HE OR SHE WOULD LIKE PRAYER. INITIALLY, YOU MAY NEED TO DO

THE MINISTERING, THEREBY SETTING THE
EXAMPLE FOR THE CLASS.

D. AT THE BEGINNING OF THE MINISTRY
TIME REMIND PARTICIPANTS ABOUT THE
FOLLOWING:

As we minister to each other, we need to recognize
that we are all fine-tuning our hearing of God's voice.
We may not hear clearly all the time, so we need to
carefully weigh any word of prophecy a class member
gives us. The following is a helpful guideline:

If it doesn't make sense, put it on the shelf. If it
contradicts what God has told you, let it drop. If your
spirit confirms it, make a note of it in your journal and
watch God bring it about.

E. ENCOURAGE HANDS-ON MINISTRY BY CLASS
MEMBERS. ALLOW THE GIFTS OF THE SPIRIT
TO MANIFEST IN DIFFERENT PEOPLE.

F. BE CAREFUL THAT ONE PERSON DOES NOT
DOMINATE THE MINISTERING.

G. CLOSE THE CLASS WITH PRAYER
A SAMPLE CLOSING PRAYER FOLLOWS:

"Father, we thank You for what You have done in our
lives today. We ask that by Your Holy Spirit You would
seal all that was accomplished. We thank You for Your
grace and mercy that enables us to walk with the Holy
Spirit and to personally know Jesus. Guard and protect
us until we meet again, and give us insight about the
readings assigned for next week. In Jesus' mighty
name, Amen.

LESSON 2

INTRODUCTION (CONTINUED)

MAIN PRINCIPLE

God greatly desires to communicate and have fellowship with us. He speaks to us in our spirit. We may hear God through an inner knowing, the inner voice and the authoritative voice of the Holy Spirit.

Introduction (Continued)

I. Let's Get Started!

A. WELCOME THE CLASS AND ENCOURAGE PARTICIPANTS TO SHARE WHAT GOD HAS BEEN DOING IN THEIR LIVES THIS PAST WEEK.

B. OPEN WITH PRAYER.

C. WORSHIP THE LORD. SHARE THE FOLLOWING WITH THE CLASS, AS THE LORD LEADS:

There are several reasons why we take class time to worship. Besides the fact that He is worthy of our praise, worship prepares our hearts to hear God better during class. It helps us get our eyes off ourselves and back on the Lord. Worship reminds us of God's love, faithfulness and awesome power.

D. READ, OR HAVE SOMEONE READ, THE MAIN PRINCIPLE FOR TODAY'S LESSON.

II. Supporting Principles — Cunningham — Chapters 1–3

FOLLOWING ARE SOME SUGGESTED QUOTES FROM THE BOOK. THE HOLY SPIRIT MAY GUIDE YOU TO SOME OTHERS THAT ARE IMPORTANT FOR YOUR CLASS TO DISCUSS.

A. Chapter 1

1. "... We can hear His voice once and still miss His best, if we don't keep on listening. After the *what* of guidance comes the *when* and the *how*. Granddad obeyed the what of his call—to preach the Gospel—but failed to seek further guidance as to how God wanted him to do that. If he had, maybe the ensuing conflicts would have been far less painful."

2. "Dad never forgot the close brush with death. He had been given a second chance, and this time he was determined to obey God's voice now, not at some point in the future when he felt more like it."

B. Chapter 2

1. "Both Dad and Mom talked about guidance. They were familiar with the 'inner voice,' at times quite audible, at other times more of an impression that came fully formed to the mind. They were familiar, too, with hearing Him speak through Scripture, and through dreams and visions. The high purpose of guidance, Dad kept saying, was to tell people about Jesus."

2. We can hear God's voice in *everyday* happenings, as in the story of the lost five-dollar bill.

3. "Getting God's leading for someone *else* is tricky. We can hear a confirming voice through another person. But if God has something important to tell you He will speak to you directly."

C. Chapter 3

Examples of getting guidance from God in this chapter include:

1. A call to preach—a *vision* of the words **"Go ye into all the world and preach the Gospel to every creature."**

2. An answer to prayer for guidance on what to preach about—in the form of a *thought*, "Preach on the temptations of Christ in the wilderness."

3. "*A quiet, insistent voice inside* told me that my life was to be more than cars or keeping up with others."

THE FOLLOWING SECTION SHOULD BE TAUGHT BY THE FACILITATOR.

III. Supporting Principles From Scripture for Hearing God's Voice

A. Scripture indicates that God does not guide us through our physical senses alone. He guides us through our spirit.

1. We were made in the likeness of God. **"So God created man in his own image, in the image of God he created them; male and female he created them" Genesis 1:27.**

2. Just as God is a three-part God—Father, Son and Holy Spirit—so we are three-part beings. **"May God himself, the God of peace, sanctify you through and through. May your spirit, soul and body be kept blameless at the coming of our Lord Jesus Christ" 1 Thessalonians 5:23.**

In Charles Solomon's *Handbook to Happiness* it states: "Drawing on the language of Scripture, we might say that man is a spirit, that he has a soul, and that he lives in a body."[1]

3. It is through our spirit that we hear God's voice. **"The Spirit himself testifies with our spirit that we are God's children" Romans 8:16**.

4. We need to make our spirits more attuned to God's voice.
   a. We train our minds through education.
   b. We train our bodies through exercise.
   c. We must train our spirits to be responsive to God's Spirit.

B. How Does God Speak?

The next 10 weeks will be a training time for the class, during which we will become more aware of God's voice. Many of us hear God's voice all the time but don't recognize it as God. We think it is our flesh or the voice of the enemy. We may not have taken the time before to understand how God speaks to us. We will learn to tune in to what God is saying to us, whether it be through an inner knowing, that still, small voice, or other ways God chooses.

1. One way God speaks to us is through an *inner knowing*. This can be a "knowing that you know" something, a holy hunch, your intuition. It can also be like having a "go ahead" signal inside with a sense of calm in your heart. It can also involve a sudden lack of peace inside.

FOR AN EXAMPLE FROM SCRIPTURE, READ **ACTS 16:6–7.**

GIVE A PERSONAL EXAMPLE OR SHARE THE FOLLOWING EXAMPLE:

A couple named Leslie and Everett were taking this **Hearing God's Voice** course and they shared a personal example of an inner knowing.

> We had been trying to become more sensitive to hearing God's voice. We were preparing to go away for the weekend to visit some relatives. It was a Friday evening and we had gotten a little behind schedule, and so we were rushing around the house trying to get ready. When we finally left, we had to drive through Denver during rush hour. Everett was getting a little tense because of the heavy traffic.
>
> We hadn't gone very far when I suddenly had this impression that we were supposed to go back home. Now, we were already late for our engagement, yet this impression kept eating at me. Finally, I turned to Everett and told him that I thought we were supposed to go back home. Much to his credit, Everett figured that God could be speaking to us. He said, "OK. If that is what you think we are supposed to do, we'll turn around and go back."
>
> We turned around and drove home. As soon as we walked into the house I realized why God had given me that inner knowing. In the hustle and bustle of trying to get out the door I had left the iron on. I had been ironing clothes for us to take on our trip and had forgotten to turn the iron off.
>
> I unplugged the iron, we praised God, and went on our way knowing that our home was safe. Can you imagine what might have happened if we had left

the iron on all weekend? This was a dramatic lesson for us in hearing God's voice.

This event makes it clear that God is concerned with every aspect of our lives. He cares about us personally; He cares about our family and even about our belongings. If we would just learn to hear the Holy Spirit's voice within us, we would not miss any of the exciting things God has in store for us.

IF THE CLASS IS RESPONSIVE TO THIS PORTION OF THE LESSON, YOU MAY WANT TO ASK IF ANYONE HAS A PERSONAL EXAMPLE OF HEARING THROUGH THE INNER KNOWING. IF SOMEONE'S ANSWER IS NOT QUITE RIGHT, DO NOT SAY ANYTHING CRITICAL. JUST SAY, "THAT IS INTERESTING," AND MOVE ON, KNOWING CLARIFICATION WILL COME IN THE FOLLOWING WEEKS.

2. Another way God can speak to us is through an *inner voice*. This is a still, small voice—a voice that is so small that sometimes when we hear it, we ignore it.

READ **1 KINGS 19:12**.

GIVE A PERSONAL EXAMPLE OF HEARING THE INNER VOICE OR SHARE THE FOLLOWING STORY.

Here is a story about a young man named Craig who was on a church softball team.

We were in a softball tournament and that night we had a game. During that day the Lord spoke softly to me—that I would get hit by the ball. Well,

I didn't pay attention to it; I just shrugged it off. I usually played outfield, but that evening they asked me to play shortstop. A player on the other team came up to bat and when he hit the ball, it took a funny bounce right in front of me. The way it bounced made it hard to catch and it hit me smack in the face. It knocked me out! When I came to, everyone was standing over me, praying for me.

Some friends brought me home and told my folks that I had been hit in the head pretty hard. My eye was swollen, bruised and already bloodshot. My mom didn't know whether to put ice or a steak on it as it was so tender to the touch. After my friends left, my mom said to me, "Craig, you must really hurt."

I said, "Yes, I do, but it is not from the pain of my eye. I hurt because God spoke to me and told me that I would get hit today, and I ignored His voice. When will I learn?" I felt worse about not listening to God than I did about my black eye. God's voice was so small. It was easy to ignore.

Many people have asked me since then, "What should you do if God says something like that to you?" I tell them, "Ask God what to do. Ask Him for protection. Ask Him for direction." There is no reason God would have said that to me unless He wanted to tell me how to protect myself. God cares very much about our bodies and He wants to speak to us, His children.

YOU MAY WANT TO ASK THE CLASS FOR A PERSONAL EXAMPLE OF HEARING AN INNER VOICE.

3. Another way God can speak to us is through an *authoritative voice*. This is a voice so loud that it makes you think everyone around you can hear it.

READ **1 SAMUEL 3:8–9A.**

GIVE A PERSONAL EXAMPLE OR SHARE THE FOLLOWING STORY.

This story is about a 20-year old man named Craig, who was playing the drums at a worship service.

> We were playing softly while different people were being prayed for. I watched as some people prayed for this one family. Then I heard a voice say, "There she is. That is the girl I want you to marry." The girl I knew God was talking about was a 13-year old girl named Stephanie. The voice I heard was so loud that I turned to see if my mom had heard it as well. The Lord had impressed me so strongly that this was to be my wife that I thought everyone had heard it.
>
> Needless to say, I kept this to myself for quite a while and I waited for God to bring this about. My family became close to Stephanie's family and I kept track of her as they moved around. It was many years before we started dating and we weren't married until she was 21.

That voice provided a strong, life-changing direction. Generally, when someone hears the authoritative voice of the Holy Spirit, it is for protection, direction, or strong instruction. Our Father is concerned about the direction of our lives. He is concerned about every aspect of our lives. All we need are ears to hear what His Spirit is saying.

YOU MAY WANT TO ASK THE CLASS
FOR PERSONAL EXAMPLES OF THE
AUTHORITATIVE VOICE OF GOD.

C. Conclusion

The following verses speak directly about our need to
hear God.

1. **"So, as the Holy Spirit says: Today, if you hear
   his voice, do not harden your hearts..." Hebrews
   3:7–8, 15; 4:7.**

   We need to keep our hearts soft toward God in order
   to hear Him.

2. **"So see to it that you do not reject Him or refuse
   to listen to and heed Him who is speaking [to you
   now]. For if they [the Israelites] did not escape
   when they refused to listen and heed Him Who
   warned and divinely instructed them [here] on
   earth [revealing with heavenly warnings His
   will], how much less shall we escape if we reject
   and turn our backs on Him Who cautions and
   admonishes [us] from heaven?" Hebrews 12:25
   (AMP).**

   Sometimes we are hesitant to hear God because we
   are afraid we won't want to do what He tells us to do.
   During this course, we will be asking God to work in
   our hearts so that we will more readily obey Him.

Again and again, the Lord calls out to us for fellowship.
Having fellowship with God is truly the purpose of hearing
His voice.

3. "He who can hear, let him listen to and heed what the Spirit says to the assemblies [churches] ... Behold, I stand at the door and knock; if anyone hears and listens to and heeds My voice and opens the door, I will come in to him and will eat with him, and he [will eat] with Me" Revelation 3:13, 20 (AMP).

4. When we are obedient to spend time waiting on the Lord and stay in fellowship with Him, we will experience Isaiah 30:21: "Whether you turn to the right or to the left, your ears will hear a voice behind you, saying, 'This is the way; walk in it.'"

IV. The main goal of this 12-week course is to learn how to hear God's guidance both at home and as we minister to one another in class. It is wonderful to see what God does as we follow His leading during the ministry time. The following are guidelines for listening to God's voice during class:

A. Let it be natural. Don't try to conjure up something.

B. Expect God to speak to you in a unique way. The way God speaks to you and works in you is different from how He works in anyone else.

C. Do not get uptight. If it seems that everyone but you is hearing God, don't worry. Instead, pray for those to whom He is speaking. 1 Corinthians 12:14–25.

D. Let God be God! Let Him speak to you when He wants and how He wants. Don't box God in—relinquish your preconceived ideas of how God leads. Relax! He is your Father and it is His desire to fellowship with you more than you can think or imagine!

V. The Discussion of the Assigned Article

ASK THE CLASS WHAT POINTS FROM THE ARTICLE IMPACTED THEM THE MOST.

VI. Next Week's Assignment

A. REVIEW NEXT WEEK'S ASSIGNMENT ON THE COURSE OUTLINE.

B. REVIEW THE MAIN PRINCIPLE FOR NEXT WEEK'S LESSON.

VII. Ministry Time

A. AS FACILITATOR, YOU NEED TO GUIDE THE MINISTRY TIME. REFER TO THE CLASS FORMAT SECTION OF THE *FACILITATOR TRAINING STUDY GUIDE* AND READ THE "MINISTRY TIME" SECTION. (Note: The *Facilitator Training Study Guide* is the booklet you received during Facilitator Training.)

B. DURING THE MINISTRY TIME, WE SUGGEST THAT YOU DO NOT ASK CLASS MEMBERS FOR THEIR PRAYER REQUESTS. SAY TO THE PARTICIPANTS, "In general, in this course we wait until Lesson 5 to begin personal prayer ministry. In Lesson 5 we will begin praying for each lesson's discussion leaders during the ministry time."

C. ON THE OTHER HAND, IF YOU SENSE THE LORD DIRECTING YOU TO ADDRESS THE NEED FOR PERSONAL PRAYER MINISTRY IN A CLASS MEMBER, ASK THE PERSON CONCERNED IF HE OR SHE WOULD LIKE PRAYER. INITIALLY, YOU MAY NEED TO DO THE MINISTERING, THEREBY SETTING THE EXAMPLE FOR THE CLASS.

D. AT THE BEGINNING OF THE MINISTRY TIME REMIND PARTICIPANTS ABOUT THE FOLLOWING:

As we minister to each other, we need to recognize that we are all fine-tuning our hearing of God's voice. We may not hear clearly all the time, so we need to carefully weigh any word of prophecy a class member gives us. The following is a helpful guideline:

If it doesn't make sense, put it on the shelf. If it contradicts what God has told you, let it drop. If your spirit confirms it, make a note of it in your journal and watch God bring it about.

E. ENCOURAGE HANDS-ON MINISTRY BY CLASS MEMBERS. ALLOW THE GIFTS OF THE SPIRIT TO MANIFEST IN DIFFERENT PEOPLE.

F. BE CAREFUL THAT ONE PERSON DOES NOT DOMINATE THE MINISTERING.

G. CLOSE THE CLASS WITH PRAYER
A SAMPLE CLOSING PRAYER FOLLOWS:

"Father, we thank You for what You have done in our lives today. We ask that by Your Holy Spirit You would seal all that was accomplished. We thank You for Your grace and mercy that enables us to walk with the Holy Spirit and to personally know Jesus. Guard and protect us until we meet again, and give us insight about the readings assigned for next week. In Jesus' mighty name, Amen.

LESSON 3

UNDERSTANDING GOD'S VOICE

MAIN PRINCIPLE

We must listen for God's voice in our spirit, and not be led astray by what others say nor depend totally on our own limited reasoning. As we hear and obey God's voice, we can participate in God's plans for the world. Following God's instructions will result in a positive impact on us and our families.

Understanding God's Voice

I. Let's Get Started!

A. WELCOME THE CLASS AND ENCOURAGE PARTICIPANTS TO SHARE WHAT GOD HAS BEEN DOING IN THEIR LIVES THIS PAST WEEK.

B. OPEN WITH PRAYER.

C. WORSHIP THE LORD. SHARE THE FOLLOWING WITH THE CLASS, AS THE LORD LEADS:

There are several reasons why we take class time to worship. Besides the fact that He is worthy of our praise, worship prepares our hearts to hear God better during class. It helps us get our eyes off ourselves and back on the Lord. Worship reminds us of God's love, faithfulness and awesome power.

D. READ, OR HAVE SOMEONE READ, THE MAIN PRINCIPLE FOR TODAY'S LESSON.

II. Supporting Principles — Cunningham — Chapters 4–6

ASK THE FOLLOWING QUESTIONS AND ENCOURAGE THE CLASS TO IDENTIFY POINTS FROM THESE CHAPTERS THAT WERE IMPORTANT TO THEM.

What methods did God use to provide guidance in these chapters? What principles of guidance were mentioned?

FOLLOWING ARE SOME SUGGESTED QUOTES FROM THE BOOK. THE HOLY SPIRIT MAY GUIDE YOU TO SOME OTHERS THAT ARE IMPORTANT FOR YOUR CLASS TO DISCUSS.

A. Chapter 4

One method God used was a vision—"a mental movie."

B. Chapter 5

1. Another method was a mental list. The Holy Spirit reminds us of truths learned in the past (**John 14:26**).

2. God can speak through Christian friends.

C. Chapter 6

1. Darlene had a vision of herself surrounded by Asian children—a call to be a missionary.

2. Darlene assumed that God didn't want her to ever marry because He had called her to be a missionary. Don't add to what God has told you.

III. Supporting Principles From Scripture — Genesis 6:5 through 8:22

Noah was a man who heard God's voice in his spirit. We look to him as an example (**1 Corinthians 10:11**). He knew God and trusted His guidance enough to carry out the impossible. Such obedience to God's voice had a radical effect on Noah and his immediate family.

A. Background (SECTIONS 1 AND 2 NEED TO BE TAUGHT.)

1. As we prepare to examine Noah's relationship with God, and how the Lord spoke to him, we must first understand how God operates. God desires for His children to understand His ways.

   The account of the flood reveals the truth that God never does anything He has not announced beforehand through His prophets. **"Surely the Sovereign Lord does nothing without revealing his plan to his servants the prophets" Amos 3:7**.

   Reveal is translated from the Hebrew word *galah* (gaw-law´), which means to uncover, unveil or disclose. In **Amos 3:7** *galah* implies the revealing of a secret.[1]

   ///

   He always prepares the hearts of His people before
   He speaks regarding a new direction.

   ///

2. So God spoke to Noah's ancestors of an impending doom and prepared Noah's heart before telling him to build the ark. God revealed His plan through His servants before Noah came on the scene. God began revealing His plans through the names of the ancestors who preceded Noah.

   a. *Jared*—**Genesis 5:18**—According to *Dake's Annotated Reference Bible* this name means "to descend or cast down... Could it be that his name was prophetical of the casting down or overthrow of the race by a deluge?"[2]

---

b. *Enoch*—means "to walk up and down, be conversant."[3] **Genesis 5:22** says that *Enoch walked with God* 300 years, starting when Methuselah was born. Perhaps something very significant happened to Enoch at this time. Perhaps God gave Enoch a revelation of what was to come. (Remember **Amos 3:7**.) This could be the reason Enoch named his son Methuselah.[4]

c. *Methuselah*—**Genesis 5:25**—means "when he is dead it (the deluge) shall come."[5] God's mercy and long-suffering is revealed by the fact that Methuselah lived 969 years. God gave people ample warning of what He would do if they continued in their evil ways.

d. *Lamech*—**Genesis 5:28**—means "destroyer." Lamech died five years before the flood that would destroy mankind on earth.[6]

e. *Noah*—**Genesis 5:29**—is similar to the Hebrew word *noach* (no´-akh), which means "rest or comfort."[7] His father said, **"He will comfort us in the labor and painful toil of our hands caused by the ground the Lord has cursed."**

Because of the preservation of a remnant of God's people in the ark, Christ was eventually born and He brought ultimate victory over evil.

///

Today, as in Noah's day, God desires to fellowship with His children. He gives direction, instructions, reproof, encouragement and, most importantly, He seeks to build an intimate relationship with them.

///

3. However, the times before God spoke to Noah were evil. Most people did not want a relationship with God.

IF PARTICIPANTS BRING UP **GENESIS 6:1-4,** WHICH MENTIONS THE **"SONS OF GOD,"** DON'T WASTE PRECIOUS TIME DISCUSSING THIS. THERE ARE SEVERAL CONFLICTING IDEAS ABOUT WHO THEY WERE AND THIS IS NOT RELATED TO THE MAIN PRINCIPLE.

a. The Lord saw that the wickedness of man was great (**Genesis 6:5**). The Hebrew word for *great* means "abundant, full, exceedingly."[8]

b. **"The Lord was grieved that He had made man on the earth, and his heart was filled with pain"** **Genesis 6:6.** *Grieved* is translated from a Hebrew word that literally means to groan; to lament because of the misery of others.[9] This verse clearly shows that God has feelings just like we do, and it causes Him great pain when He sees His creation being twisted and perverted by sin.

c. The Lord wanted to destroy the human race from the face of the earth (**Genesis 6:7**). Mankind's relationship with God was one of rejection because of their great wickedness.

4. However, unlike mankind who contended with God's Spirit, Noah found favor in the eyes of the Lord (**Genesis 6:3, 8**).

Noah found favor in God's eyes because:

a. He was a righteous man (**Genesis 6:9; 7:1**). *Righteous* in Hebrew means "blameless, mature, or well rounded, though not sinless."[10]

b. He walked with God (**Genesis 6:9**). Like his ancestor Enoch, Noah had a relationship with God.

c. He preached righteousness. God **"protected Noah, a preacher of righteousness, and seven others ..." 2 Peter 2:5**. Noah followed in the footsteps of his great-grandfather, Enoch, who also preached righteousness (**Genesis 5:24; Jude 14–16**).

B. God spoke to Noah.

1. The Lord gave Noah specific guidance (**Genesis 6:11–21**).

a. The following quote comes from the *Ryrie Study Bible—NAS*:

The ark by today's measurements was 450 ft. long, 75 ft. broad, and 45 ft. high, with a displacement of about 20,000 tons and gross tonnage of about 14,000 tons. Its carrying capacity equaled that of 522 standard railroad stock cars [each of which can hold 240 sheep]. Only 188 cars would be required to hold 45,000 sheep-sized animals, leaving three trains of 104 cars each for food, Noah's family, and "range" for the animals.[11]

b. God told Noah to take his family into the ark and to take with him clean and unclean animals (**Genesis 7:2**). God told him to take seven pairs of "clean" animals so that some could be used for sacrifices (**8:20**) and one pair of "unclean" animals for reproduction (**6:19; 7:2**). (This indicates a knowledge of clean and unclean animals before the law of Moses as found in **Leviticus 11** and **Deuteronomy 14**.)[12]

2. The case of Noah shows that the Lord does reveal his secrets to his prophets because God spoke directly and specifically to Noah about the coming flood.

3. Today the Lord reveals things to us. In **John 15:15** Jesus said to his disciples, **"I no longer call you servants, because a servant does not know his master's business. Instead, I have called you friends, for everything that I learned from my Father I have made known to you."**

C. **Noah must have perceived God's instructions in his spirit (or inner man).**

1. These verses are not clear as to how Noah heard God, whether through an inner voice or authoritative voice, etc., but he was able to hear because of his close relationship with God. He was so tuned in to God's voice.

2. Noah heard God in his spirit, not his intellect. He didn't perceive these instructions in his intellect because they didn't make sense. They defied reason.

When God speaks to you, it won't always make sense at first.

3. God's instructions encouraged Noah's faith. **"By faith Noah, when warned about things not yet seen, in holy fear built an ark to save his family. By**

his faith he condemned the world and became heir of the righteousness that comes by faith" Hebrews 11:7.

///

When God speaks to you, it will increase your faith.

///

D. God asked Noah to do the impossible—and then enabled him to do it.

1. Noah had one week to load the ark (**Genesis 7:4, 10**).

2. As Noah believed, God enabled the animals to come to him (**Genesis 6:20; 7:8–9, 15**).

3. Once Noah heard God in his spirit, he didn't allow his mind or his neighbors to dissuade him because Noah believed God would enable him (**Genesis 6:22; 7:5**).

///

When God tells us to do something, He helps us do it.

///

E. God fulfilled His words and carried out His plans.

1. In **Genesis 7:4** the Lord said to Noah, **"Seven days from now I will send rain on the earth for forty days and forty nights, and I will wipe from the face of the earth every living creature I have made."**

2. It came to pass. **"And after the seven days the floodwaters came on the earth" Genesis 7:10.**

   a. **"The springs of the great deep"** mentioned in **Genesis 7:11** apparently means that subterranean waters, as well as rain, contributed to the flood.

b. **"Then the Lord shut him in" Genesis 7:16**. The Lord closed the door of the ark behind Noah and his family. A supernatural act is indicated. God must have opened the door after the flood, too (**Genesis 8:16**).

F. "But God remembered Noah..." Genesis 8:1.

1. *The NIV Study Bible* comments on the word *remember*: "So far the flood narrative has been an account of judgment; from this point on it is a story of redemption... To 'remember' in the Bible is not merely to recall to mind; it is to express concern for someone, to act with loving care for him."[13]

2. The Hebrew word for *remembered* is *zakar* (zaw-kar´), which also means "to be mindful of a covenant."[14] God was remembering the covenant He had made with Noah and his family in **Genesis 6:18**. The same word is used again in **Genesis 9:15** when God promised to remember His covenant with Noah and all living creatures.

G. Noah cooperated with God's plans—Genesis 8:4–21

1. Once the ark had come to rest on Mount Ararat, Noah sent out the raven and then the dove to determine how wet the ground was and whether the animals could survive outside the ark.

2. Noah sent out a raven. Ravens are scavengers that will eat dead fish and frogs, refuse, and small animals "like mussels and clams."[15] They have no qualms about perching on a slimy surface. Noah's raven apparently had no trouble finding food, as it did not return to the ark (**Genesis 8:7**).

3. He then sent out a dove.

    a. The dove serves as a symbol of holiness and purity. It prefers not to land on a wet, slimy surface. It is not a scavenger and will not eat carrion (dead animals), which would have been plentiful as the waters receded. Doves eat seeds, fruit, grains and insects.[16] Noah's dove returned to the ark, having found no place to land and no food. **Genesis 8:9** says that Noah **"reached out his hand and took the dove and brought it back to himself in the ark."**

    b. Noah waited seven more days and sent the dove out a second time. This time the dove returned with an olive leaf in its beak. Noah took the dove back into the ark and waited another seven days. The third time Noah sent out the dove, the dove did not return (**Genesis 8:12**).

4. This passage where Noah sends out and receives the dove serves as a symbol of God the Father and the Holy Spirit. *The ark represents the dwelling place of the Father. Noah might represent God the Father, gently and lovingly sending forth the dove, the Holy Spirit,* and gently and lovingly bringing the dove back into a place of rest, into His presence.

    a. The first time Noah sent out the dove can be compared to when the Father sent His Spirit to people in the Old Testament. In those days kings, priests and other individuals had an anointing of the Holy Spirit for a particular job. The Holy Spirit would come upon that person for a period of time, but then the Spirit would go back to the Father.

b. The second time Noah sent out the dove can be compared to when the Father sent the Holy Spirit to Jesus in the form of a dove at Jesus' baptism (**Luke 3:22**). In **Luke 4:1**, when Jesus was led into the desert, He is described as **"full of the Holy Spirit."** When Jesus walked the earth, He had the Holy Spirit in Him without measure. But when Jesus died, resurrected and ascended into heaven, He took the Spirit back with Him. Then the Father welcomed Jesus and the Holy Spirit back into His presence, just as Noah welcomed the dove carrying the olive leaf back into the ark. (The olive branch is a symbol of peace; Jesus is known as the Prince of Peace in **Isaiah 9:6**.)

c. After Jesus ascended into heaven He asked the Father to send the Spirit, the Comforter, to be with His disciples so that He would be with them and in them forever. The third time Noah sent out the dove can be compared to when the Father sent the Holy Spirit to be with Jesus' disciples. Like Jesus after His baptism, we can have the fullness of the Holy Spirit within us (**Ephesians 5:18**). And until Christ's second coming, the Holy Spirit will remain with us and in us, and not return to the Father.

5. Noah moved within God's timing (waited for a word from God).

a. He built the ark when God told him to, even though it made no sense to his neighbors (**Genesis 6:22**).

b. He waited when it seemed unnecessary to wait by not sending out the dove for another seven days (**Genesis 8:12**).

c. He moved when God said to move (**Genesis 8:15–18**).

d. Noah and his family stayed in the ark for more than a year!

H. God's response to obedience

1. Our study opened with God expressing great pain and regret that He had created man and it closes with God being pleased with Noah's obedience and worship. **"The Lord smelled the pleasing aroma..." Genesis 8:21**.

2. Noah is a good example of an obedient man.

   a. He acted in obedience, even though he didn't fully understand. The idea of a flood covering the whole earth would not be easily grasped by anyone at that time.

   b. Noah allowed what he heard from God in his spirit to determine his actions—he built the ark.

3. Noah's awareness of God speaking in his spirit and his willingness to follow that guidance had dramatic implications for Noah and his family.

   a. God made a covenant with Noah (**Genesis 6:18**).

   b. God saved Noah and his family from sure doom (**Matthew 24:37–39**).

   c. Trusting God and following His instructions— including the what, how and when—will result in a positive impact on us and our families. God promises to bless the families of those who obey Him (**Psalm 112:1–2; Jeremiah 32:38–39**).

4. God looks for people, like Noah, whose hearts belong to Him. **"For the eyes of the Lord range throughout the earth to strengthen those whose hearts are fully committed to him" 2 Chronicles 16:9a.**

//

God delights in communicating with us through His Holy Spirit inside us, but it is up to us to keep our hearts teachable and sensitive to His leading.

//

IV. Discussion of the Assigned Article

ENCOURAGE SEVERAL CLASS MEMBERS TO SHARE SOME MAIN POINTS FROM THE ASSIGNED ARTICLE.

V. Next Week's Assignment

A. REVIEW NEXT WEEK'S ASSIGNMENT ON THE COURSE OUTLINE.

B. REVIEW THE MAIN PRINCIPLE FOR NEXT WEEK'S LESSON.

C. ASSIGN A DISCUSSION LEADER FOR THE BOOK DISCUSSION IN LESSON 5, EITHER NOW OR NEXT WEEK. A FACILITATOR WILL LEAD THE SCRIPTURE DISCUSSION.

NOTE TO THE FACILITATOR
YOU NEED TO CALL OR VISIT THE LESSON 5 DISCUSSION LEADER DURING THE WEEK BEFORE THAT CLASS. SEE THE APPENDIX

FOR QUESTIONS YOU CAN USE DURING
THIS CONVERSATION TO HELP THE LEADER
PREPARE FOR THIS CLASS. REMEMBER TO CALL
THE DISCUSSION LEADERS DURING THE WEEK
BEFORE EACH LESSON.

VI. Ministry Time

A. AS FACILITATOR, YOU NEED TO GUIDE
THE MINISTRY TIME. REFER TO THE CLASS
FORMAT SECTION OF THE *FACILITATOR
TRAINING STUDY GUIDE* AND READ THE
"MINISTRY TIME" SECTION. (Note: The *Facilitator
Training Study Guide* is the booklet you received during
Facilitator Training.)

B. DURING THE MINISTRY TIME, WE SUGGEST
THAT YOU DO NOT ASK CLASS MEMBERS
FOR THEIR PRAYER REQUESTS. SAY TO THE
PARTICIPANTS, "In general, in this course we wait
until Lesson 5 to begin personal prayer ministry.
In Lesson 5 we will begin praying for each lesson's
discussion leaders during the ministry time."

C. ON THE OTHER HAND, IF YOU SENSE THE
LORD DIRECTING YOU TO ADDRESS THE
NEED FOR PERSONAL PRAYER MINISTRY
IN A CLASS MEMBER, ASK THE PERSON
CONCERNED IF HE OR SHE WOULD LIKE
PRAYER. INITIALLY, YOU MAY NEED TO DO
THE MINISTERING, THEREBY SETTING THE
EXAMPLE FOR THE CLASS.

D. AT THE BEGINNING OF THE MINISTRY TIME REMIND PARTICIPANTS ABOUT THE FOLLOWING:

As we minister to each other, we need to recognize that we are all fine-tuning our hearing of God's voice. We may not hear clearly all the time, so we need to carefully weigh any word of prophecy a class member gives us. The following is a helpful guideline:

If it doesn't make sense, put it on the shelf. If it contradicts what God has told you, let it drop. If your spirit confirms it, make a note of it in your journal and watch God bring it about.

E. ENCOURAGE HANDS-ON MINISTRY BY CLASS MEMBERS. ALLOW THE GIFTS OF THE SPIRIT TO MANIFEST IN DIFFERENT PEOPLE.

F. BE CAREFUL THAT ONE PERSON DOES NOT DOMINATE THE MINISTERING.

G. CLOSE THE CLASS WITH PRAYER

LESSON 4

SPIRIT, SOUL, BODY–WHAT'S THE DIFFERENCE?

MAIN PRINCIPLE

Since we hear God's voice in our spirit, we need to understand the differences between the spirit, soul and body.

LESSON 4

Spirit, Soul, Body — What's the Difference?

I. Let's Get Started!

A. WELCOME THE CLASS AND ENCOURAGE PARTICIPANTS TO SHARE WHAT GOD HAS BEEN DOING IN THEIR LIVES THIS PAST WEEK.

B. OPEN WITH PRAYER.

C. WORSHIP THE LORD. SHARE THE FOLLOWING WITH THE CLASS, AS THE LORD LEADS:

There are several reasons why we take class time to worship. Besides the fact that He is worthy of our praise, worship prepares our hearts to hear God better during class. It helps us get our eyes off ourselves and back on the Lord. Worship reminds us of God's love, faithfulness and awesome power.

D. READ, OR HAVE SOMEONE READ, THE MAIN PRINCIPLE FOR TODAY'S LESSON.

HIGHEST PRIORITY TIME-WISE SHOULD BE GIVEN TO SECTION III — TEACHING: SPIRIT, SOUL, BODY — WHAT'S THE DIFFERENCE?

II. Supporting Principles — Cunningham — Chapters 7–9

ASK THE FOLLOWING QUESTIONS AND
ENCOURAGE THE CLASS TO IDENTIFY POINTS
FROM THESE CHAPTERS THAT WERE IMPORTANT
TO THEM.

What methods did God use to provide guidance in these
chapters? What principles of guidance were mentioned?

FOLLOWING ARE SOME SUGGESTED QUOTES
FROM THE BOOK. THE HOLY SPIRIT MAY GUIDE
YOU TO SOME OTHERS THAT ARE IMPORTANT
FOR YOUR CLASS TO DISCUSS.

A. Chapter 7

1. Darlene had to directly hear from God what her role in the ministry would be.

2. The Lord told Darlene to speak to a "boy in a green sweater." Because Darlene was obedient, Don was sure God wanted him to go on the Summer of Service.

3. God provided the people needed for this Summer of Service. When God directs us to do something, He provides what we need to accomplish it.

B. Chapter 8

1. As the kids obeyed God by going on the mission trip, God used them to bless others—ministering salvation and healing to many.

2. During the storm that battered the island, Cunningham was directed to address both parts of the Gospel message: to teach people to love God with all their hearts, souls, minds, and strength (evangelism), and to love one's neighbors as one's self by doing acts of mercy for people.

As we follow God's direction, we will find ourselves sharing the Gospel message with people, as well as helping meet their nonspiritual needs.

3. God can guide by causing an idea to take shape in your mind, e.g., having a ship bring needed material help to those with whom you are sharing the gospel.

C. Chapter 9

1. The closed door from his denomination caused Cunningham to move into God's plan for his life.

   a. God may not show us the whole picture at first, but we need to stay true to what God has told us to do.

   b. A result of obeying God's voice can be disapproval from others.

2. Be totally submitted to the Holy Spirit and let Him use any tool He chooses to speak to you. This may include Him giving you a chapter and verse from the Bible, or telling you and other Christians the same thing as you ask Him a question together.

3. God brought to mind the Bible passage in which Jesus fasted and prayed in the wilderness, in order to tell Cunningham to do something similar.

4. God confirmed this by directing the Dawsons to invite him to stay with them.

III. Teaching: Spirit, Soul, Body — What's the Difference?

WE RECOMMEND THAT YOU REFER TO THE ZOE WEBSITE, WWW.ZOEMINISTRIES.ORG, FOR THE LESSON 4 TEACHING OF "SPIRIT, SOUL, BODY— WHAT'S THE DIFFERENCE?" YOU CAN USE THIS VIDEO TO HELP YOU PREPARE TO PRESENT THIS MATERIAL, OR IF YOU PREFER, YOU MAY PLAY IT FOR YOUR CLASS.

THIS SECTION IS AN EXCEPTION TO THE RULE OF "DON'T JUST TEACH" THE MATERIAL. HAVE THE CLASS REFER TO THE **"SPIRIT, SOUL, BODY—WHAT'S THE DIFFERENCE? OUTLINE TO ACCOMPANY TEACHING"** FOUND IN THEIR STUDY GUIDE AS YOU TEACH THIS SECTION.

A. Introduction

1. It is an awesome reality that the God of the universe desires to communicate with each of us. In fact, in **Jeremiah 33:3** God challenges us: **"Call to me and I will answer you and tell you great and unsearchable things you do not know!"**

   a. The Hebrew word for *call* is *qara* (kaw-raw´), which means to cry out, to call to someone, to call upon, to ask aid—especially of God. This term is used for any kind of cry, even a cry not articulated.[1]

b. The Hebrew word for *unsearchable* is *batsar* (baw-tsar´), which means isolated or inaccessible. The idea here is that God will reveal to us things we do not know or things hidden to the casual observer. For example, He can show us the most effective way to pray for specific people or situations.[2]

2. God wants to fellowship with us! Even before we were born again, God was drawing us to Himself by His Spirit.

///

After being born again, God Almighty takes residence within us. He lives within our spirits by His Holy Spirit. The Holy Spirit communicates to our spirit what God is saying.

///

3. God's communication with us can be compared to a radio station. Just as a radio station constantly transmits a signal for your radio to receive, so the Lord is constantly sending communication to us. Our spirit is the receiver of God's signals. However, too often our soul causes static—like a radio that is not exactly tuned to the station. The static created by our soul prevents us from hearing God's voice clearly.

Here's an example: You may have an impulse to talk to someone you don't know, but not knowing it is God directing you, you question the idea and don't follow the impulse. Here your soul (your reasoning of why you shouldn't talk to a stranger) overrides your spirit and you miss a chance to show God's love to that person. Obedience comes more easily when you *recognize* that it is God's voice directing you. So in the next three lessons we will try to fine-tune our spirit so that we can hear God speaking to us more clearly.

B. Man Is a Three-part Being

Man is made in God's image (**Genesis 1:26–27**). God is a three-part God, consisting of the Father, Son and Holy Spirit. Man is a three-part being with a spirit, soul and body. **"May God himself, the God of peace, sanctify you through and through. May your whole spirit, soul and body be kept blameless at the coming of our Lord Jesus Christ" 1 Thessalonians 5:23**.

The following definitions will help us see the difference between our three parts:

1. *Spirit* in Greek is *pneuma* (pnyoo´-mah), which means breath, spirit or spiritual.[3]

    a. *Pneuma* is that part of a person capable of responding to God. **John 4:24** says, **"God is spirit and his worshipers must worship in spirit and in truth."**

    b. The spirit is where God's life and vitality, *zoe*, resides within us. Immortality is implied by the word *pneuma*.[4]

///

The spirit of a Christian can be guided by the Holy Spirit in a variety of ways and He often communicates rather quietly.

///

    c. The different ways God can communicate with us through our spirit will be covered more in depth in later lessons.

2. *Soul* in Greek is *psuche* (psoo-khay´), which is that part of us that holds our natural ability to perceive and feel.[5]

//

The soul is comprised of the mind, will and emotions,
so the soul communicates through our thoughts,
intentions and feelings.

//

a. A related Greek word is *psuchikos* (psoo-khee-kos´),
which means soulish; not possessing the Holy
Spirit; dominated by the merely physical, worldly or
natural life.[6] The characteristics of the soul can be
either positive or negative.

b. The soul promotes "self"—as in *self-awareness, self-esteem* and *self-pity*.

c. In short, it is the very essence of who we are apart
from Christ. Before we accept Christ our soul
rules us. This may continue into our Christian walk
because it is the only way we know.

3. *Body* in Greek is *sarx* (sarx), which is translated flesh,
carnal, or outer man. It is the house we live in, our
physical body.[7]

//

The body communicates through our physical senses,
appetites and lusts.

//

4. The word *heart* is also used in Scripture. It comes
from the Greek word *kardia* (kar-dee´-ah), which is
described in *The Eerdmans Bible Dictionary* as the core of
an individual. This term can indicate a person's mind,
will and emotions, but the heart is also said to motivate
and drive the mind, will and emotions. The redeemed
heart is the dwelling place of Christ.[8] So, one could
say that the heart contains the spirit and the soul.

a. The word *heart* has been used interchangeably for the spirit or the soul in both the New and Old Testaments.

"I will give you a new heart and put a new spirit in you; I will remove from you your heart of stone and give you a heart of flesh" Ezekiel 36:26.

"The good man brings good things out of the good stored up in his heart, and the evil man brings evil things out of the evil stored up in his heart. For out of the overflow of his heart his mouth speaks" Luke 6:45.

b. The mouth and the heart are connected. What we speak shows what is in our heart.

"With the tongue we praise our Lord and Father and with it we curse men, who have been made in God's likeness. Out of the same mouth come praise and cursing" James 3:9–10a.

A modern day example follows: You are driving in a car and are listening to praise music and worshiping the Lord. Suddenly a driver cuts you off and you get mad and curse him. One minute you are praising God, the next moment you are cursing someone.

The heart can have spiritual or soulish qualities. We have a choice to let the Holy Spirit fill our hearts so that the overflow of our hearts is spiritual.

C. Differentiating between the Spirit and Soul

Many people think the soul and spirit are the same, but it *is possible* to tell which is which.

1. **"For the word of God is living and active. Sharper than any double-edged sword, it penetrates even to the division of soul and spirit, joints and marrow; it judges the thoughts and attitudes of the heart" Hebrews 4:12.**

   The double-edged sword mentioned here by the author of **Hebrews** could be the sword used by a Roman soldier. It was a formidable weapon because it was short, sharp and very effective. This verse is saying that the Word of God can be very effective in differentiating between the spirit and the soul.

   Scripture can help us determine whether what we hear is coming from our soul (our mind, will or emotions), or whether it is coming from God through our spirit. Simply put, if what we hear does not line up with the Word of God, it is not from God.

2. READ **1 CORINTHIANS 15:45–49.**
   Verse 45 says, **"So it is written: 'The first man Adam became a living being; the last Adam [Jesus], a life-giving spirit.'"**

   a. In this passage we see the normal order of things. First you have the "natural" and then comes the "spiritual." We are born a natural human being. We come into this world and our soul rules us. Our mind, will and emotions are our guides. We do whatever feels good or seems right to us.

b. After we invite Jesus into our life, our spirit becomes born again. God's Spirit then lives within us to help us become like Jesus. God uses His Word to show us how to separate the soulish nature from the spiritual nature and make possible God's transformation of us into the likeness of Christ.

3. READ **MATTHEW 10:34–39**.
"Whoever finds his life will lose it, and whoever loses his life for my sake will find it" Matthew 10:39. The word *life* here is *psuche*, which refers to our soulish life, our own way of doing things with our own interests in mind. When we are willing to lose our soulish life for Jesus' sake, then we find life.

The following paraphrase of this verse is helpful: **"He who has found his soul-life, shall ruin and render it useless, and he who has passed a sentence of death upon his soul-life for my sake shall find it" Matthew 10:39** *(The New Testament–An Expanded Translation)*.

4. We can allow our thoughts and actions to be governed either by our soul or by our spirit, in which the Holy Spirit dwells.

The following verse shows we have a choice to make: **"I have set before you life and death, blessings and curses. Now choose life, so that you and your children may live and that you may love the Lord your God, listen to his voice, and hold fast to him" Deuteronomy 30:19–20a.**

D. Characteristics of the Soul and the Spirit

1. READ **JAMES 3:13–18**.

   In **verse 15** the word *unspiritual* is used and it is translated from the Greek word *psuchikos*.

   Characteristics of the soul are earthly, unspiritual, devilish, envious, and having selfish ambition, disorder, and every evil practice (**verses 15–16**).

   Characteristics of the Spirit-led spirit are pure, peace-loving, considerate, submissive, full of mercy and good fruit, impartial, and sincere (**verses 17–18**).

2. READ **JUDE 17–21**.

   In **verse 19** the word *natural* is used and is translated from the Greek word *psuchikos*.

   Characteristics of the soul are ungodly desires and division in the Body of Christ (**verses 18–19**).

   Characteristics of the spirit are holy faith and God's love (**verses 20–21**).

3. READ **1 CORINTHIANS 2:7–16**.

   In **verse 14** we read about **"the man without the Spirit."** In *The King James Version* this verse reads **"the natural man,"** and *natural* is translated from the Greek word *psuchikos*.

A characteristic of the soul is having spiritual things seem foolish (**verse 14**). When we let our soul rule us, the things of the Spirit can seem foolish to our own mind.

Characteristics of the spirit include God's wisdom (**verses 7, 13**), the ability to judge (or "appraise" in NAS) all things, and having the mind of Christ (**verses 15–16**). We can know the deep things of God and we can have the mind of Christ when we allow our spirit to rule us because we have the Holy Spirit indwelling our spirit!

E. How do we Fine-tune our Spirit and Eliminate the Static of the Soul?

1. With God's Word—**James 1:21**

   "Therefore, get rid of all moral filth and the evil that is so prevalent and humbly accept the word planted in you, which can save you." In *The King James Version* this last phrase reads **"is able to save your soul,"** which is translated from the Greek word *psuche*.

   The New Living Bible reads, **"So get rid of all that is wrong in your life, both inside and outside, and humbly be glad for the wonderful message we have received, for it is able to save our souls as it takes hold of our hearts"** James 1:21.

2. With Prayer—**Matthew 26:36–46**

   In the Garden of Gethsemane Jesus' soul (*psuche*) was overwhelmed with sorrow and He wanted to avoid what He knew was the Father's will for Him. **"My Father, if it is possible, may this cup be taken from me"** (**verses 38–39**). Sometimes our soul struggles with what God is asking us to do. Jesus recognized the struggle between the soul and spirit and continued in prayer (three times) until He had victory. After prayer He was ready to walk in obedience (**verse 45**).

3. With Praise—**Psalm 57:6–11**

The psalmist's soul was downcast but he chose to praise God. Praise gets our attention on how great God is and takes our attention away from ourselves. For example, giving thanks is a sure-fire way to deal with self-pity.

F. Areas of the Soul to Bring into Submission

1. The *mind* is logical and likes to argue and reason things out. We can be double-minded, torn between the soul and the spirit, wavering back and forth on an issue.

   The Word of God is the answer.

   READ **JAMES 1:5–8**. As we read scripture, the Holy Spirit gives us wisdom and helps bring our mind into submission to God. The Spirit of God is not doubled-minded.

2. The *will* can be very strong and out of God's will sometimes. It can set an agenda that is not God's plan, or it can be impatient and not wait for God's timing.

   Prayer is the answer when your will is out of line with God's will.

   If we delight ourselves in God and converse with Him,

His desires become our desires (**Psalm 37:4–6**).

If we abide with God through prayer and meditation on what He has said, we can patiently wait for God to do it in His own time and way (**John 15:7**).

3. The *emotions* are swayed by circumstances. If circumstances are bad, we can get discouraged and forget what God has told us.

Praise is the answer.

"Why are you downcast, O my soul? Why are you so disturbed within me? Put your hope in God, for I will yet praise him, my Savior and my God" Psalm 42:5.

Therefore:

If your *mind* is giving you trouble, spend time in the *Word*.

If your *will* is giving you trouble, spend time in *prayer*.

If your *emotions* are the problem, spend time *praising God*.

G. Summary

1. **"Come to me all you who are weary and burdened, and I will give you rest. Take my yoke upon you and learn from me, for I am gentle and humble in heart, and you will find rest for your souls. For my yoke is easy and my burden is light"** Matthew 11:28–30.

When we are being led by our soul we will feel weary and burdened. When we are led by our spirit we will be gentle and humble, and find rest for our mind, will and emotions.

2. A Spirit-led spirit
   a. Confirms the Word of God
   b. Brings life
   c. Provides rest
   d. Gives glory to God

3. A Soul not in submission to God
   a. Contradicts Scripture or uses it out of context
   b. Leads to death
   c. Takes effort
   d. Gives glory to man

4. When our will is leading, there is a driving, pushing force. Satan has influence over our soul realm. Satan pushes; the Holy Spirit leads.

//

Moving from being led by the soul to being led by the spirit is like shifting your weight from one foot to the other while skiing. The motion is subtle, but the outcome is amazingly different.

//

5. **"Since we live by the Spirit, let us keep in step with the Spirit" Galatians 5:25.** When we walk in the Spirit we will be motivated by God's mind, will and emotions rather than only our own.

6. As you choose to submit to your spirit, which is being governed by the Holy Spirit, God will guide you and bless you as He uses your mind, will and emotions for His good purposes and to His glory.

IV. Discussion of the Assigned Article

ASK CLASS MEMBERS TO SHARE WHAT POINTS IMPACTED THEM THE MOST FROM THE ARTICLE.

V. Next Week's Assignment

A. REVIEW NEXT WEEK'S ASSIGNMENT ON THE COURSE OUTLINE.

B. REVIEW THE MAIN PRINCIPLE FOR NEXT WEEK'S LESSON.

C. ASSIGN DISCUSSION LEADERS FOR LESSON 6, EITHER NOW OR NEXT WEEK: ONE TO LEAD THE SCRIPTURE DISCUSSION AND ANOTHER THE BOOK AND ARTICLE DISCUSSIONS.

D. ASK PARTICIPANTS TO PRAY FOR NEXT WEEK'S DISCUSSION LEADER DURING THE WEEK AND BE READY TO PRAY FOR HIM OR HER NEXT WEEK. ENCOURAGE THEM TO ASK GOD FOR SCRIPTURES OR WORDS OF ENCOURAGEMENT OR EXHORTATION FOR THE DISCUSSION LEADER.

IF THIS IS NEW TO YOUR CLASS, YOU MIGHT USE THE FOLLOWING EXPLANATION:

> The idea of asking God for Scripture verses or words of encouragement for someone else may be new to you. We are just taking God at His word in **Jeremiah 33:3: "Call to me and I will answer you and tell you great and unsearchable things you do not know."** We can call on God and ask Him to give us Scripture verses or words of encouragement that He wants the discussion leaders to hear from Him. Don't be discouraged if you don't get something for each person. Your responsibility is to give God the time and opportunity to communicate with you—the rest is up to God.

NOTE TO THE FACILITATOR
YOU NEED TO CALL OR VISIT THE LESSON
5 DISCUSSION LEADERS DURING THE WEEK
BEFORE THAT CLASS. SEE THE APPENDIX FOR
QUESTIONS YOU CAN USE DURING THESE
CONVERSATIONS TO HELP THE LEADERS
PREPARE FOR THIS CLASS. REMEMBER TO
CALL THE DISCUSSION LEADERS DURING
THE WEEK BEFORE *EACH* LESSON.

VI. Ministry Time

A. AS FACILITATOR, YOU NEED TO GUIDE THE
MINISTRY TIME. REFER TO THE ZOE CLASS
FORMAT SECTION OF THE *FACILITATOR
TRAINING STUDY GUIDE* AND READ THE
"MINISTRY TIME" SECTION. (Note: The *Facilitator
Training Study Guide* is the booklet you received during
Facilitator Training.)

B. DURING THE MINISTRY TIME, WE SUGGEST
THAT YOU DO NOT ASK CLASS MEMBERS
FOR THEIR PRAYER REQUESTS. SAY TO THE
PARTICIPANTS, "In general, in this course we wait
until Lesson 5 to begin personal prayer ministry.
In Lesson 5 we will begin praying for *each* lesson's
discussion leaders during the ministry time."

C. ON THE OTHER HAND, IF YOU SENSE THE
LORD DIRECTING YOU TO ADDRESS THE
NEED FOR PERSONAL PRAYER MINISTRY
IN A CLASS MEMBER, ASK THE PERSON
CONCERNED IF HE OR SHE WOULD LIKE
PRAYER. INITIALLY, YOU MAY NEED TO DO

THE MINISTERING, THEREBY SETTING THE
EXAMPLE FOR THE CLASS.

D. AT THE BEGINNING OF THE MINISTRY
TIME REMIND PARTICIPANTS ABOUT THE
FOLLOWING:

As we minister to each other, we need to recognize that
we are all fine-tuning our hearing of God's voice. We
may not hear clearly all the time, so we need to carefully
weigh any word of prophecy a class member gives us.
The following is a helpful guideline:

If it doesn't make sense, put it on the shelf. If it
contradicts what God has told you, let it drop. If your
spirit confirms it, make a note of it in your journal and
watch God bring it about.

E. ENCOURAGE HANDS-ON MINISTRY BY CLASS
MEMBERS. ALLOW THE GIFTS OF THE SPIRIT
TO MANIFEST IN DIFFERENT PEOPLE.

F. BE CAREFUL THAT ONE PERSON DOES NOT
DOMINATE THE MINISTERING.

G. CLOSE THE CLASS WITH PRAYER.

LESSON 5

SPIRIT, SOUL, BODY– WHO RULES?

MAIN PRINCIPLE

We have the choice of listening to our spirit, which is directed by the Holy Spirit, or to our soul. Sometimes the soul can make it hard to hear and obey what God is saying in our spirit.

Spirit, Soul, Body — Who Rules?

I. Let's Get Started!

A. WELCOME THE CLASS AND ENCOURAGE PARTICIPANTS TO SHARE WHAT GOD HAS BEEN DOING IN THEIR LIVES THIS PAST WEEK.

B. OPEN WITH PRAYER.

C. WORSHIP THE LORD. SHARE THE FOLLOWING WITH THE CLASS, AS THE LORD LEADS:

There are several reasons why we take class time to worship. Besides the fact that He is worthy of our praise, worship prepares our hearts to hear God better during class. It helps us get our eyes off ourselves and back on the Lord. Worship reminds us of God's love, faithfulness and awesome power.

D. READ, OR HAVE SOMEONE READ, THE MAIN PRINCIPLE FOR TODAY'S LESSON.

II. Supporting Principles — Cunningham — Chapters 10 and 11

What principles of guidance were mentioned in these chapters?

FOLLOWING ARE SOME SUGGESTED QUOTES FROM THE BOOK. THE HOLY SPIRIT MAY GUIDE YOU TO SOME OTHERS THAT ARE IMPORTANT

FOR YOUR CLASS TO DISCUSS.

A. Chapter 10

1. Undergoing "soul surgery"—repenting when God brings up sinful thoughts, attitudes or actions—can provide a way for clearer communication with God. "We hear the Lord more clearly if we come to Him with a clean heart."

2. "If this idea of a school for teaching the ways of the Lord really came from God, then it was reasonable to expect that He'd give it to more than one person." — The Wise Men Principle.

3. "Incredibly, Dar told me that she had been fasting and praying on the same exact days as I, and that she, too, had gone through soul surgery."

4. God can confirm an idea as coming from Him by speaking of it again to you, perhaps in more depth, and by using The Wise Men Principle—in this case, telling the same idea to the Bible teacher, Willard Cantelon.

B. Chapter 11

1. "Being transparently honest before God and before man was necessary if we were to make progress hearing God's voice. I'd seen for myself how God's power was released after a time of cleansing... The cleansing season had set me free—the devil had none of my secret resentments and sins to hold over me anymore."

2. "Confession to man brings humility and unity and makes a repentant person ready to receive God's healing of mind, emotion and body. Confession is good for the soul."

3. "Guidance, like prophecy, has one tough criterion for validity: Does it work?"

III. Supporting Principles From Scripture—
Genesis 15:1–6
Genesis 16:1–12
Genesis 17:15–21
Genesis 21:1–21

A. Preview

The purpose of this section is to allow Scripture to further define the difference between our spirit and soul. The questions on the study help **"Spirit, Soul, Body— Who Rules?"** can serve as a springboard for discussion of this passage.

Sarai is God's choice to be the mother of the promised child. We would submit to you that Sarai can represent the spirit. This is not to say that Sarai always did right. However, she was *the way God chose* to give Abram a son. Hagar, who was *man's way* of bringing about the promise, represents the soul.

///

Our spirit, when led by the Holy Spirit, will cooperate
with God's plan for our life.

///

B. Genesis 15:1–6

1. The Lord revealed to Abram His plan to give Abram a son. God's plan was already Abram's desire. **"Delight yourself in the Lord and He will give you the desire of your heart" Psalm 37:4**.

2. Abram believed what God told him. READ **Romans 4:16–22**. Abraham was fully **"persuaded that God had power to do what he had promised" Romans 4:21**.

C. Genesis 16:1–12

1. When we don't see God's plan coming about in our life, we may choose to help God out, which is what Sarai did in **verses 1–3**. Our soul gains leadership over our spirit when we rely on our own effort instead of believing and waiting on the Lord.

2. **Verse 4**—Hagar began to despise her mistress. A spiritual equivalent could be that as our soul continues to rule over our spirit, the things of the Spirit will become devalued or despised in our eyes. For example, time spent in the Word and in prayer on a busy day may seem to be a waste of precious time to our soul, even though our spirit knows that our time with God is where we get our strength and guidance (**1 Corinthians 2:14**).

3. **Verse 5**—Even though Sarai was the one to suggest that Abram produce an heir through Hagar, Sarai blamed Abram for her suffering. As things go wrong for us, we may cry out to God, "How could You let this happen to me?" However, sometimes things go awry because we were led by our soul.

4. **Verse 6**—Just as Abram told Sarai she was in control of her maid, so we can allow our spirit to rule us.

5. **Verses 6–8**—Like Hagar, our soul may resist the discipline of our spirit and "feel" mistreated, e.g., how we sometimes feel while fasting.

6. **Verse 9**—God told Hagar to go back and submit to Sarai. In the same way, our soul needs to submit to the authority of our spirit!

7. **Verses 10–11**—Just as the angel of the Lord cared for Hagar, so God hears and cares for the needs of our soul.

8. **Verse 12**—Notice the similarity between Ishmael's and the soul's characteristics.

D. Genesis 17:15–21

1. In **verses 5** and **15** God changed Abram's and Sarai's names. The name change was representative of the covenant God was establishing with them. He promised to make Abraham the father of many and Sarah the mother of nations and kings.

2. **Verses 15–16**—The Lord restated and expanded upon His plan for Abraham and Sarah.

3. **Verse 17**—Abraham laughed and doubted when God said that 90-year-old Sarah would give him a son. Again, this is equivalent to the things of the Spirit seeming like foolishness to our soul.

4. **Verses 18–19**—Even after God promised to produce the promised heir through Sarah, Abraham wanted

God to bless Ishmael, who was produced outside of God's plan. After realizing God's plan for us, we often have a tendency to say, "But what about how I feel or what I want, Lord?" When we are promoting our own plan, the Lord's answer to us is: "No."

5. **Verses 19–21**—God's covenant or plan for us is revealed to us by the Holy Spirit in our spirit.

///

God's blessing rests on our soul when we are walking in obedience to Him with our soul in submission to the Spirit of God within us.

///

E. Genesis 21:1–21

1. **Verses 1–2**—God fulfilled His word to Abraham. God always fulfills His word to us (**Numbers 23:19**).

2. **Verses 6–7**—Sarah experienced great joy from the birth of Isaac. There is joy in serving the Lord (**Nehemiah 8:10**).

3. **Verse 9**—Just as the son of Hagar mocked the son of Sarah, so our soul will continue to mock or resist our spirit (**James 3:15–16**).

4. **Verse 10**—Sarah recognized that there would always be a conflict between Ishmael and Isaac. Our spirit and our soul cannot rule together; only one may be in leadership.

5. **Verse 11**—Abraham was distressed that his son Ishmael might suffer. Disciplining our soul can bring us distress.

6. **Verses 12–13**—God promised to bless Ishmael if Abraham did what Sarah suggested. When our spirit walks in obedience to the Holy Spirit within us, God will bless our soul as well.

7. **Verse 14**—It must have been painful for Abraham to send Hagar and Ishmael away. For us, obedience may also seem painful.

8. **Verses 15–16**—Just as Hagar was sure they were going to die, so our soul may feel as if it is going to die while submitting to our spirit.

9. **Verses 17–21**—God heard the boy crying. God hears the cries of our soul, too! He meets all of our needs (**Philippians 4:19**).

IV. Next Week's Assignment

A. REVIEW NEXT WEEK'S ASSIGNMENT ON THE COURSE OUTLINE.

B. REVIEW THE MAIN PRINCIPLE FOR NEXT WEEK'S LESSON.

C. ASSIGN DISCUSSION LEADERS FOR LESSON 7, EITHER NOW OR NEXT WEEK: ONE TO LEAD THE SCRIPTURE DISCUSSION AND ANOTHER THE BOOK AND ARTICLE DISCUSSIONS.

D. ASK PARTICIPANTS TO PRAY FOR NEXT WEEK'S DISCUSSION LEADERS DURING THE WEEK AND BE READY TO PRAY FOR THEM IN CLASS. ENCOURAGE THEM TO ASK GOD FOR SCRIPTURES OR WORDS OF ENCOURAGEMENT OR EXHORTATION FOR THEM.

IF THIS IS NEW TO YOUR CLASS, YOU MIGHT USE THE FOLLOWING EXPLANATION:

The idea of asking God for Scripture verses or words of encouragement for someone else may be new to you. We are just taking God at His word in **Jeremiah 33:3: "Call to me and I will answer you and tell you great and unsearchable things you do not know."** We can call on God and ask Him to give us Scripture verses or words of encouragement that He wants the discussion leaders to hear from Him. Don't be discouraged if you don't get something for each person. Your responsibility is to give God the time and opportunity to communicate with you—the rest is up to God.

NOTES TO THE FACILITATOR:
YOU NEED TO CALL OR VISIT THE LESSON 6 DISCUSSION LEADERS DURING THE WEEK BEFORE THAT CLASS. SEE THE APPENDIX FOR QUESTIONS YOU CAN USE DURING THESE CONVERSATIONS TO HELP THE LEADERS PREPARE FOR THIS CLASS. REMEMBER TO CALL THE DISCUSSION LEADERS DURING THE WEEK BEFORE *EACH* LESSON.

ASK THE CLASS WHICH WEEK WILL WORK BEST FOR HAVING THE POTLUCK MEAL TOGETHER (USUALLY AFTER LESSON 6 OR 7).

AS PARTICIPANTS BEGIN LEADING DISCUSSIONS AND BECOMING INVOLVED DURING THE MINISTRY TIME, THEY MAY WANT TO TELL OTHERS ABOUT WHAT GOD IS DOING IN THE LIVES OF CLASS MEMBERS. PLEASE REMIND THEM TO KEEP CONFIDENTIAL SENSITIVE PERSONAL INFORMATION SHARED IN CLASS.

V. Ministry Time

A. AS FACILITATOR, YOU NEED TO GUIDE THE MINISTRY TIME. REFER TO THE CLASS FORMAT SECTION OF THE *FACILITATOR TRAINING STUDY GUIDE* AND READ THE "MINISTRY TIME" SECTION. (Note: The *Facilitator Traning Study Guide* is the booklet you received during Facilitator Training.)

B. BE SURE TO PRAY FOR THIS WEEK'S DISCUSSION LEADERS. ENCOURAGE PARTICIPANTS TO SHARE ANY SCRIPTURES OR WORDS OF ENCOURAGEMENT THAT THE LORD GAVE FOR THESE LEADERS.

C. NOTE: THE MINISTRY EMPHASIS HAS NOW SHIFTED TO THE WEEKLY DISCUSSION LEADERS. ANY OTHER PERSONAL MINISTRY SHOULD NOW BE ADDRESSED AFTER CLASS UNLESS THE HOLY SPIRIT STRONGLY DIRECTS YOU OTHERWISE.

D. AT THE BEGINNING OF THE MINISTRY TIME REMIND PARTICIPANTS ABOUT THE FOLLOWING:

As we minister to each other, we need to recognize that we are all fine-tuning our hearing of God's voice. We may not hear clearly all the time, so we need to carefully weigh any word of prophecy a class member gives us. The following is a helpful guideline:

If it doesn't make sense, put it on the shelf. If it contradicts what God has told you, let it drop. If your spirit confirms it, make a note of it in your journal and watch God bring it about.

E. ENCOURAGE HANDS-ON MINISTRY BY CLASS MEMBERS. ALLOW THE GIFTS OF THE SPIRIT TO MANIFEST IN DIFFERENT PEOPLE.

Generally, we minister with our eyes open, so we can see how the person to whom we are ministering is doing. It is most important to have the compassion of the Lord when we minister, wanting solely to bless that person. Usually, only men touch men, and only women should lay hands on women. If you feel led to touch someone of the opposite sex, a hand on the back of the shoulder might be appropriate. Otherwise, have someone of the same gender touch the person, and you place your hand over theirs. We want to be sensitive to the person who is receiving ministry.

F. BE CAREFUL THAT ONE PERSON DOES NOT DOMINATE THE MINISTERING.

G. CLOSE WITH PRAYER. (See sample prayer on p. 31)

LESSON 6

OBEYING THE SPIRIT

MAIN PRINCIPLE

As we learn to obey the Holy Spirit, we will become more aware of how the Holy Spirit can minister through us.

Obeying the Spirit

I. Let's Get Started!

A. WELCOME THE CLASS AND ENCOURAGE PARTICIPANTS TO SHARE WHAT GOD HAS BEEN DOING IN THEIR LIVES THIS PAST WEEK.

B. OPEN WITH PRAYER.

C. WORSHIP THE LORD. SHARE THE FOLLOWING WITH THE CLASS, AS THE LORD LEADS:

There are several reasons why we take class time to worship. Besides the fact that He is worthy of our praise, worship prepares our hearts to hear God better during class. It helps us get our eyes off ourselves and back on the Lord. Worship reminds us of God's love, faithfulness and awesome power.

D. READ, OR HAVE SOMEONE READ, THE MAIN PRINCIPLE FOR TODAY'S LESSON.

II. Supporting Principles—Cunningham Chapters 12 and 13 and Points 1 and 2

FOLLOWING ARE SOME SUGGESTED QUOTES FROM THE BOOK. THE HOLY SPIRIT MAY GUIDE YOU TO SOME OTHERS THAT ARE IMPORTANT FOR YOUR CLASS TO DISCUSS.

A. Chapter 12

1. "The Lord will lead us into victory, but success itself is the most dangerous obstacle to hearing properly the voice of God."

2. "I thought back over the past two years and how easily things had been happening. We had found the formula and it was working! 'It's all there, for any Christian to discover,' I reminded myself, perhaps a bit cockily. 'Just get the word of the Lord on what He wants to do, declare His word aloud, and then watch it happen.'"

   Cockiness or pride can creep in following success and prevent God from using you fully.

3. "God, if You're saying now is the time to begin [pursuing the ship], please help me to be certain. Taking on something this big would cost us dearly."

   When you are used to having circumstances go well as you obey God and carry out a specific job, you may not recognize God's leading in another direction if that path seems tough.

B. Chapter 13

1. "...500 under my leadership would stay back at the castle getting replenished with lots of teaching, prayer and Bible reading."

   Rest, prayer and Scripture study are essential to hearing God's voice.

2. "I somehow knew just what the ship would be like: about 500 feet long, able to sleep several hundred, a floating campus for a school, and having large cargo holds able to carry materials to needy people."

The inner knowing can be a "knowing that you know" something.

3. "When the third individual told me about an inter-island ferry named the Maori for sale in New Zealand, I began to take notice."

God may confirm what He has told you through other people.

C. Points 1 and 2

1. Point 1—If you obey God and stay humble, He promises to guide you.

2. Point 2—Obedience requires a heart yielded to God. "There is a direct link between yieldedness and hearing."

III. Supporting Principles From Scripture — 2 Chronicles 19:1–11 2 Chronicles 20:1–30

A. Background—2 Chronicles, Chapters 14–18

1. Background on Jehoshaphat's father, King Asa.

   a. King Asa did what was right in the eyes of the Lord by destroying the places for worshiping other gods. He commanded the people of Judah to seek the

Lord and obey God's laws (**2 Chronicles 14:2–4**).

b. Azariah went out to meet Asa and said to him, **"Listen to me, Asa and all Judah and Benjamin. The Lord is with you when you are with Him. If you seek him, he will be found by you, but if you forsake him, he will forsake you"** 2 Chronicles 15:2.

What a promise—and what a warning! Many other Scriptures confirm that God is free to bless those who seek after Him with all their heart (**Jeremiah 29:13–14; 2 Chronicles 16:9**). When we become entangled in worldly matters and are half-hearted in our walk with the Lord, we are still His children, but our fellowship and communion with the Lord is greatly hampered.

c. King Asa obeyed God until the 36th year of his reign. It was then that Asa made a treaty with the king of Aram to protect himself from the king of Israel. Asa's successful reign faltered at this point and he became enraged at Hanani, the seer, who boldly told him that he had failed to trust God and that there would be consequences (**2 Chronicles 16:7–9**).

2. Background on King Jehoshaphat

a. Jehoshaphat was a bold follower of God, as was his father in the early part of his reign (**2 Chronicles 17:3–6**).

b. Because of Jehoshaphat's relationship with God, the Lord was with him (**2 Chronicles 17:3**).

c. **"His heart was devoted to the ways of the Lord ..." 2 Chronicles 17:6.** *The King James Version* reads, **"And his heart was lifted up in the ways of the Lord...."** The Hebrew verb used here means to take pride in, to elevate, to exalt to a greater degree of dignity and honor.[1] Jehoshaphat's desire was to see God honored and obeyed.

d. Jehoshaphat established that God's law was to be the law of the land (**2 Chronicles 17:9**).

e. As a result of Jehoshaphat's obedience and respect of God's law, the fear of the Lord fell on all the kingdoms that were around Judah, and Jehoshaphat became increasingly powerful (**2 Chronicles 17:10, 12**).

f. Although Jehoshaphat was deeply committed to God, he arranged for his son to marry Athaliah, the daughter of wicked King Ahab of Israel and his wife, Jezebel (**2 Chronicles 18:1**).

   Jehoshaphat's popularity and power attracted the cunning, opportunistic Ahab. Their alliance had devastating consequences.

   • Jehoshaphat almost lost his life by going into battle with Ahab (**2 Chronicles 18:29–31**).

   • Jehoshaphat incurred God's wrath (**2 Chronicles 19:2**).

   • When Jehoshaphat died and then his succeeding son died, wicked Athaliah became queen. She seized the throne and almost destroyed all of David's descendants (**2 Chronicles 22:10**). This would have prevented Jesus from being born to Mary.

- Athaliah brought the evil practices of Israel into Judah, which eventually led to the nation's downfall.

B. Principles of Obeying—2 Chronicles 19:1 through 20:30

1. Jehoshaphat put God's word first and encouraged others to do the same (**2 Chronicles 18:4** and **2 Chronicles 19:3**).

2. He inquired of the Lord and fasted before doing anything (**2 Chronicles 20:1–4**).

3. Jehoshaphat prayed, acknowledging God's power and his own powerlessness, and he entreated God's mercy (**2 Chronicles 20:6–12**).

4. He listened to what the Spirit was saying through the prophet, Jahaziel (**2 Chronicles 20:14–17**).

5. Jehoshaphat obeyed God's instructions (**2 Chronicles 20:20–22**).

    a. He waited for the proper time. The Lord had said, **"Tomorrow march down against them"** **2 Chronicles 20:16**.

    b. He told the people, **"Have faith in the Lord your God and you will be upheld; have faith in his prophets and you will be successful"** **2 Chronicles 20:20**. In *The King James Version* it reads, **"Believe in the Lord your God, so shall**

ye be established; believe his prophets, so shall ye prosper."

Believing in God's instructions is as important as *obedience.*

Believe in Hebrew is `*aman* (aw-man´), which means to be firm, steadfast; to trust and be certain. A derivative of this term is *amen,* which means "So be it!"[2]

We need to believe that if we obey God's instructions, He will do what He has said He would do.

    c. After he had inquired of the Lord and prayed, He then consulted with the people. They agreed that God seemed to be promising His favor, protection and victory (**2 Chronicles 20:21**).

    d. So, Jehoshaphat carried out the plan God had given them. They started marching down against their enemy, ready to take up their positions and stand firm. And, most importantly, Jehoshaphat appointed men to sing praises to the Lord as they marched out and were **"not afraid or discouraged" 2 Chronicles 20:15–17.**

C. Results of Obeying—2 Chronicles 20:22–30

    1. God acts on our behalf.

As Jehoshaphat began to sing and to praise God with the expectancy that He would fight for them, their enemies were defeated (**2 Chronicles 20:22–23**).

//

God inhabits the praises of His people (**Psalm 22:3 KJV**).
Whenever and wherever God's people praise Him, He is there
among them and does miraculous things on their behalf.

//

2. God will give us favor and prosperity in the ministry
   He has ordained for each of us.

   God gave Jehoshaphat victory both in the eyes of men
   and in God's eyes. Jehoshaphat and his men carried
   off much plunder (**2 Chronicles 20:24–25**).

3. God will be glorified.

   After Jehoshaphat and his men saw what God had
   done for them, they worshiped and praised God
   (**2 Chronicles 20:26–28**).

4. Obedience to God will bring peace and rest
   (**2 Chronicles 20:29–30**).

IV. Discussion of the Assigned Articles

ASK CLASS MEMBERS TO SHARE WHAT THEY
LEARNED FROM EACH ARTICLE.

V. Next Week's Assignment

A. REVIEW NEXT WEEK'S ASSIGNMENT ON THE
COURSE OUTLINE.

B. REVIEW THE MAIN PRINCIPLE FOR NEXT
WEEK'S LESSON.

C. STRESS THE IMPORTANCE OF THE PARTICIPANTS GOING THROUGH THE LIST OF HINDRANCES TO HEARING GOD ON THE STUDY HELP **"WHAT KEEPS US FROM HEARING GOD'S VOICE."** ENCOURAGE THEM TO ASK GOD TO POINT OUT WHICH OF THESE HINDRANCES HE WANTS THEM TO DEAL WITH AT THIS TIME. ENCOURAGE THEM TO PAY SPECIAL ATTENTION TO THE SCRIPTURES UNDER THAT SPECIFIC HINDRANCE.

D. ASSIGN DISCUSSION LEADERS FOR LESSON 8, EITHER NOW OR NEXT WEEK: ONE CLASS MEMBER FOR THE SCRIPTURE DISCUSSION AND ANOTHER TO LEAD THE BOOK AND ARTICLE DISCUSSIONS.

E. REMIND PARTICIPANTS TO PRAY FOR NEXT WEEK'S DISCUSSION LEADERS DURING THE WEEK AND BE READY TO PRAY FOR THEM IN CLASS. ENCOURAGE THEM TO ASK GOD FOR SCRIPTURES OR WORDS OF ENCOURAGEMENT OR EXHORTATION.

VI. Ministry Time

A. AS FACILITATOR, YOU NEED TO GUIDE THE MINISTRY TIME. REFER TO THE CLASS FORMAT SECTION OF THE *FACILITATOR TRAINING STUDY GUIDE* AND READ THE "MINISTRY TIME" SECTION. (Note: The *Facilitator Training Study Guide* is the booklet you received during Facilitator Training.)

B. BE SURE TO PRAY FOR THIS WEEK'S DISCUSSION LEADERS. ENCOURAGE PARTICIPANTS TO SHARE ANY SCRIPTURES OR WORDS OF ENCOURAGEMENT THAT THE LORD GAVE FOR THESE LEADERS.

C. NOTE: THE MINISTRY EMPHASIS HAS NOW SHIFTED TO THE WEEKLY DISCUSSION LEADERS. ANY OTHER PERSONAL MINISTRY SHOULD NOW BE ADDRESSED AFTER CLASS UNLESS THE HOLY SPIRIT STRONGLY DIRECTS YOU OTHERWISE.

D. INITIALLY, YOU MAY NEED TO DO THE MINISTERING, THEREBY SETTING THE EXAMPLE FOR THE CLASS.

E. AT THE BEGINNING OF THE MINISTRY TIME REMIND PARTICIPANTS ABOUT THE FOLLOWING:

As we minister to each other, we need to recognize that we are all fine-tuning our hearing of God's voice. We may not hear clearly all the time, so we need to carefully weigh any word of prophecy a class member gives us. The following is a helpful guideline:

If it doesn't make sense, put it on the shelf. If it contradicts what God has told you, let it drop. If your spirit confirms it, make a note of it in your journal and watch God bring it about.

F. ENCOURAGE HANDS-ON MINISTRY BY CLASS MEMBERS. ALLOW THE GIFTS OF THE SPIRIT TO MANIFEST IN DIFFERENT PEOPLE.

Generally, we minister with our eyes open, so we can see how the person to whom we are ministering is doing. It is most important to have the compassion of the Lord when we minister, wanting solely to bless that person. Usually, only men touch men, and only women should lay hands on women. If you feel led to touch someone of the opposite sex, a hand on the back of the shoulder might be appropriate. Otherwise, have someone of the same gender touch the person, and you place your hand over theirs. We want to be sensitive to the person who is receiving ministry.

G. BE CAREFUL THAT ONE PERSON DOES NOT DOMINATE THE MINISTERING.

H. CLOSE WITH PRAYER.

LESSON 7

WHAT KEEPS US FROM HEARING GOD'S VOICE

MAIN PRINCIPLE

As we seek to hear God's voice more clearly, we will need to keep our hearts yielded toward the Lord. Sin in our life acts as a barrier to communication with God.

What Keeps Us From Hearing God's Voice?

I. Let's Get Started!

A. WELCOME THE CLASS AND ENCOURAGE PARTICIPANTS TO SHARE WHAT GOD HAS BEEN DOING IN THEIR LIVES THIS PAST WEEK.

B. OPEN WITH PRAYER.

C. WORSHIP THE LORD. SHARE THE FOLLOWING WITH THE CLASS, AS THE LORD LEADS:

There are several reasons why we take class time to worship. Besides the fact that He is worthy of our praise, worship prepares our hearts to hear God better during class. It helps us get our eyes off ourselves and back on the Lord. Worship reminds us of God's love, faithfulness and awesome power.

D. READ, OR HAVE SOMEONE READ, THE MAIN PRINCIPLE FOR TODAY'S LESSON.

II. Supporting Principles From Scripture—
1 Samuel 10:1–10
1 Samuel 13:1–14
1 Samuel 15:1–35
1 Samuel 16:1–13

A. Background

1. Up to this time the Israelites had been led by prophets, priests and judges, with Samuel being the most recent. Now in **1 Samuel 8** they complained and said they wanted a king like everyone else. Samuel was displeased. In **1 Samuel 8:7–8** God told Samuel, **"It is not you they have rejected, but they have rejected me as their king. As they have done from the day I brought them up out of Egypt until this day, forsaking me and serving other gods, so they are doing to you."**

2. In **1 Samuel 8:10–18** Samuel warned the people against having a king. **"When that day comes, you will cry out for relief from the king you have chosen, and the Lord will not answer you in that day" 1 Samuel 8:18.**

3. But the people refused to listen and insisted on having a king. **"Then we will be like all the other nations, with a king to lead us and to go out before us and fight our battles" 1 Samuel 8:20.**

   So often in the Body of Christ people want others to tell them what to do. They don't want to take the time to get a hold of God and ask Him about the situations in their own lives.

4. So, God instructed Samuel to anoint Saul as king. In **1 Samuel 9** we get an idea of who Saul was. We learn that he came from the tribe of Benjamin and he was **"an impressive young man without equal among the Israelites—a head taller than any of the others" 1 Samuel 9:2**.

5. God pointed out Saul as the man He wanted Samuel to anoint as king (**1 Samuel 9:17**).

6. When Samuel indicated that Saul was to be Israel's leader, Saul reacted with surprise. **"But am I not a Benjamite, from the smallest tribe of Israel, and is not my clan the least of all the clans of the tribe of Benjamin? Why do you say such a thing to me?"** 1 Samuel 9:21.

   Saul did *not* see himself as other people did—as **"an impressive young man without equal among the Israelites."**

B. 1 Samuel 10:1–10

1. In this chapter Samuel anointed Saul as Israel's king. Samuel predicted what would happen to Saul after they parted company. Among other things, Samuel told Saul that he would encounter a procession of prophets who were prophesying. **"The Spirit of the Lord will come upon you in power, and you will prophesy with them; and you will be changed into a different person. Once these signs are fulfilled, do whatever your hand finds to do, for God is with you"** verses 6–7.

   As Saul left Samuel, God changed Saul's heart. **"The Spirit of God came upon him in power, and he joined in their prophesying"** verse 10.

2. God equipped Saul for the position in which He placed him. Saul had all that he needed to be a good king. He certainly looked like a king physically, but, more importantly, God placed the Holy Spirit on Saul.

Saul's heart changed into the heart God wanted him to have.

///

Similarly, God has equipped us with what we need to do the job He has given each of us. He has placed His Spirit in us. All we need to do is follow the leading of the Holy Spirit in our spirit and keep our heart yielded toward God.

///

C. 1 Samuel 13:1–14

1. The scene in this chapter was the preparation for a battle between Israel and the Philistines. Saul's forces were greatly outnumbered and they were quaking with fear.

2. Earlier Samuel had told Saul to wait for him at Gilgal (**1 Samuel 10:8**). Samuel, the priest, was to sacrifice burnt offerings and fellowship offerings there.

3. However, Saul allowed his soul to rule him and he acted in disobedience:

   a. He became impatient and did not wait for Samuel as he had been instructed earlier (**1 Samuel 10:8**).

   b. He should not have sacrificed the burnt offerings. It showed arrogance on Saul's part to take up the role of priest without being anointed by God (**verse 9**).

   c. He gave in to fear of being killed by the Philistines and fear of disapproval from his men (**verses 8–9**).

   d. He wanted to get God's blessing and favor before the battle by sacrificing the offerings, but he wasn't willing to obey God (**verse 12**).

4. Like Saul, we can become weary of waiting when we don't see the Lord doing what He said He would do. We can become impatient and decide to implement our own plans.

5. In **verses 13–14** Samuel rebuked Saul for his disobedience. Saul missed God's best for him because of his rebellion. Samuel said, **"He would have established your kingdom over Israel for all time. But now your kingdom will not endure; the Lord has sought out a man after his own heart and appointed him leader of his people, because you have not kept the Lord's command."**

There is no mention of Saul repenting of his disobedience.

Verse 14 makes it clear that the reason Saul was being rebuked by Samuel was because of his heart attitude. David was the man whom God was now appointing king because David's heart was right before God.

D. 1 Samuel 15:1–35

1. In the beginning of this chapter the Lord was perfectly clear about what He wanted Saul to do. He wanted the Amalekites and everything associated with them completely destroyed because of what they had done to the Israelites when they came out of Egypt.

2. Saul's rebellion started with not killing Agag, the Amalekite king. Then Saul and his soldiers kept the best of the Amalekite livestock, destroying only the weaker animals (**verse 9**).

   The Amalekites serve as a type for sin (**Exodus 17:16**). Not destroying all of the Amalekites and their possessions is like repenting of most sins but harboring one little secret sin.

3. God grieved because Saul had turned away from Him and knowingly disregarded His instructions (**verse 11**). The word *grieved* gives us a sense of how deeply hurt God was by Saul's disobedience.

4. We see evidence of the change in Saul's heart since the time he was anointed king. In **verse 12** Saul went to Carmel to set up a monument in *his own honor.* What arrogance!

   Saul's arrogance was evidenced first by his trying to operate in the role of a priest, then defying the word of the Lord to kill the Amalekites and their livestock, and finally setting himself up in a place of honor.

5. Saul compounded his guilt by lying in **verse 13. "The Lord bless you! I have carried out the Lord's instructions."** Once confronted with his disobedience, Saul did not repent but tried to shift the blame onto his men. **"They spared the best of the sheep ... but <u>we</u> totally destroyed the rest" verse 15**. God considered Saul's partial obedience as *disobedience.*

6. In **verse 17** Samuel said, **"Although you were once small in your own eyes, did you not become the head of the tribes of Israel? The Lord anointed you king over Israel."** After all God had done for him, Saul allowed his men to **"pounce on the plunder and do evil in the eyes of the Lord" verse 19.**

Saul's deep-seated feelings of inferiority caused him to not stand up to his men. He should have ordered them to do as the Lord had directed.

///

To God, feelings of inferiority are no excuse for disobedience.

///

7. In **verse 20** Saul lied again and then tried to justify his sparing the best livestock by rationalizing that they intended to sacrifice them to God. Notice Saul said **"the Lord your God" verse 21**. Saul's heart had turned away from the Lord.

8. Samuel told it like it was in **verses 22–23**. He said, **"Does the Lord delight in burnt offerings and sacrifice as much as in obeying the voice of the Lord? To obey is better than sacrifice, and to heed is better than the fat of rams."** Samuel pointed out Saul's sins of rebellion, arrogance and disobedience.

9. Saul admitted that he had sinned because he was afraid of the people. He allowed them to influence him and he feared their disapproval more than God's disapproval (**verse 24**).

10. Even after God rejected him as king, he was mostly concerned with his reputation. **"I have sinned. But please honor me before the elders of my people and before Israel; come back with me, so that I may worship the Lord your God" verse 30**.

11. Saul intended to go on as if nothing had happened! Saul was being led by his soul.

His heart became harder and harder toward the instructions of God and he did not walk in the fear of the Lord.

///

We must not be led by our soul—by our logic, emotions or our own desires. Instead, we should walk in the fear of the Lord, obeying God and not being swayed by fear of disapproval from other people.

///

E. 1 Samuel 16:1–13

1. In this chapter Samuel secretly anointed David as king at God's command. God told him in **verse 7b**, **"The Lord does not look at the things man looks at. Man looks at the outward appearance, but the Lord looks at the heart."** In looking at the psalms that David wrote, we can see that he loved God.

2. We know from Scripture that David sinned many times in his life, but each time he earnestly repented and kept his heart clean before God.

///

God delights in our obedience. He desires to commune with us through our spirit. It is up to us to keep our heart soft and pliable, sensitive and obedient to the leading of the Holy Spirit.

///

III. Study Help "What Keeps Us From Hearing God's Voice?"

A. HAVE PARTICIPANTS LOOK AT THIS SHEET. ASK IF THEY HAD ANY QUESTIONS WHEN THEY WENT OVER THIS STUDY HELP. A BRIEF EXPLANATION OF EACH ITEM FOLLOWS:

1. *Not spending time with the Lord—in prayer, the Word and worship*
   If we are too busy to spend time with God, we will miss what He's trying to say to us through these three main avenues of communication.

   a. Prayer is talking with God. So, after we have poured out our heart to Him, we need to give God a chance to speak to us.

   b. The Bible is a major tool God uses to communicate with us. He can cause certain verses to leap off the page so that we know what He is wanting to tell us.

   c. Worship—both corporate and personal. As we come to Him in adoration, He responds by revealing what is on His heart.

2. *Walking in unforgiveness*
   Holding a grudge against someone acts like a ceiling between us and the Lord. It can feel as if our prayers are bouncing off that ceiling back at us.

3. *Unconfessed sin*
   Unconfessed sin in our life acts as a barrier between us and our holy God. **"If I had cherished sin in my heart, the Lord would not have listened..." Psalm 66:18.** When we have secret sin in our life and we don't allow the Holy Spirit to deal with that sin, we won't hear much from God.

4. *Unbelief*
   If we don't believe that God can speak to us, we won't hear Him. Unbelief can keep us from walking by faith and hearing further guidance.

5. *Fear*
Walking in fear of man (people) will limit hearing and obeying God. Fear of coming into God's presence because of feelings of unworthiness or not wanting to hear what He has to say can also prevent us from hearing Him.

6. *Lack of knowledge*
We need to know *how* God speaks to us in order to hear Him clearly and consistently. God speaks through His Word, His people and His Spirit into our spirit.

7. *Not being truly born again or filled with the Spirit*
We need the Holy Spirit indwelling us to hear Him in our spirit. Once we are filled with the Spirit, our minds and hearts understand God's Word in a new way.

B. Did a certain item on the list leap off the page at you when you read it? Consider the Scriptures that go with your problem area. Ask God to help you deal with it, so that you can hear His voice more clearly.

IV. Discussion of the Assigned Articles

ASK THE CLASS WHAT PARTS OF EACH ARTICLE GOD USED MOST TO SPEAK TO THEM.

V. Next Week's Assignment

A. REVIEW NEXT WEEK'S ASSIGNMENT ON THE COURSE OUTLINE.

B. REVIEW THE MAIN PRINCIPLE FOR NEXT WEEK'S LESSON.

C. ASK PARTICIPANTS TO LOOK IN THE BOOK AND SCRIPTURE READING ASSIGNMENTS FOR: 1) PRINCIPLES OF GUIDANCE, AND 2) EXAMPLES OF THE INNER KNOWING. REFER THEM TO THE ARTICLE **"INNER KNOWING."**

D. ASSIGN DISCUSSION LEADERS FOR LESSON 9, EITHER NOW OR NEXT WEEK: ONE CLASS MEMBER FOR THE SCRIPTURE DISCUSSION AND ANOTHER TO LEAD THE BOOK AND ASSIGNED ARTICLE DISCUSSIONS.

E. REMIND PARTICIPANTS TO PRAY FOR NEXT WEEK'S DISCUSSION LEADERS DURING THE WEEK AND BE READY TO PRAY FOR THEM IN CLASS AND ENCOURAGE THEM TO ASK GOD FOR SCRIPTURES OR WORDS OF ENCOURAGEMENT OR EXHORTATION FOR THEM.

VI. Ministry Time

A. AS FACILITATOR, YOU NEED TO GUIDE THE MINISTRY TIME. REFER TO THE CLASS FORMAT SECTION OF THE *FACILITATOR TRAINING STUDY GUIDE* AND READ THE "MINISTRY TIME" SECTION. (Note: The *Facilitator Training Study Guide* is the booklet you received during Facilitator Training.)

B. IF THE LORD DIRECTS YOU TO HAVE A TIME OF REPENTANCE, IT MIGHT BE HELPFUL TO PLAY SOME MUSIC TO PROVIDE MORE PRIVACY.

C. BE SURE TO PRAY FOR THIS WEEK'S DISCUSSION LEADERS. ENCOURAGE PARTICIPANTS TO SHARE ANY SCRIPTURES OR WORDS OF ENCOURAGEMENT THAT THE LORD GAVE FOR THESE LEADERS.

D. NOTE: THE MINISTRY EMPHASIS HAS NOW SHIFTED TO THE WEEKLY DISCUSSION LEADERS. ANY OTHER PERSONAL MINISTRY SHOULD NOW BE ADDRESSED AFTER CLASS UNLESS THE HOLY SPIRIT STRONGLY DIRECTS YOU OTHERWISE.

E. AT THE BEGINNING OF THE MINISTRY TIME REMIND PARTICIPANTS ABOUT THE FOLLOWING:

As we minister to each other, we need to recognize that we are all fine-tuning our hearing of god's voice. We may not hear clearly all the time, so we need to carefully weigh any word of prophecy a class member gives us. The following is a helpful guideline:

If it doesn't make sense, put it on the shelf. If it contradicts what God has told you, let it drop. If your spirit confirms it, make a note of it in your journal and watch God bring it about.

F. ENCOURAGE HANDS-ON MINISTRY BY CLASS MEMBERS. ALLOW THE GIFTS OF THE SPIRIT TO MANIFEST IN DIFFERENT PEOPLE.

G. BE CAREFUL THAT ONE PERSON DOES NOT DOMINATE THE MINISTERING.

H. CLOSE WITH PRAYER.

LESSON 8

DIFFERENT WAYS GOD SPEAKS – INNER KNOWING

MAIN PRINCIPLE

The inner knowing is a common way God leads us. It can take the form of a "knowing that you know," a holy hunch, a sudden uneasiness, a sense of peace or a caution.

Different Ways God Speaks — Inner Knowing

I. Let's Get Started!

A. WELCOME THE CLASS AND ENCOURAGE PARTICIPANTS TO SHARE WHAT GOD HAS BEEN DOING IN THEIR LIVES THIS PAST WEEK.

B. OPEN WITH PRAYER.

C. WORSHIP THE LORD.

D. READ, OR HAVE SOMEONE READ, THE MAIN PRINCIPLE FOR TODAY'S LESSON.

II. Definition of Inner Knowing

REVIEW THE DEFINITION ON THE ASSIGNED ARTICLE **"INNER KNOWING"** AND SHARE THE FOLLOWING ADDITIONAL INFORMATION.

A. The *inner knowing* is a common way God speaks to His children. Inner knowing can come in the form of:

1. *An intuition, a knowing that you know something, or a holy hunch.*

2. *A calm or peace that indicates that you have God's "go ahead."* When God wants you to do something, He will give you a go ahead signal. Initially, your mind might come up with reasons not to do it, but the more you pray about it, the better you feel about it inside.[1]

3. *An uneasiness or a hesitation that should cause you to stop and reassess the situation.*

   If God doesn't want you to do something, He will communicate to you through your spirit with a stop signal or a sense of uneasiness.[2] Your mind may tell you it is good or the right thing to do. But if you listen to that inner knowing, you will stay in God's will.

4. *A caution—a signal to wait.*

   God may be saying that you are not to do it just *now*; the timing is not right.

B. Remember the example of the inner knowing from Lesson 2 when Leslie and Everett had left the iron on and the Lord directed them to turn their car around and go home. Leslie had a sudden lack of peace and felt that they were supposed to go back. The inner knowing in this instance came in the form of a sudden uneasiness.

C. In some situations it may require some waiting on the Lord to have that inner knowing. If you don't know what to do, then you need to take time alone to pray and wait on God.[3] Don't allow yourself to be pushed into making a decision when you don't have a clear inner knowing from God.

///

The inner knowing is just as supernatural as guidance through visions or dreams. An inner knowing is just not as spectacular.[4]

///

III. Supporting Principles — Cunningham — Chapters 14–15 and Points 3, 4 and 5

FOLLOWING ARE SOME SUGGESTED QUOTES FROM THE BOOK. THE HOLY SPIRIT MAY GUIDE YOU TO SOME OTHERS THAT ARE IMPORTANT FOR YOUR CLASS TO DISCUSS.

What principles of guidance were mentioned in these chapters?

A. Chapter 14

1. "I was, however, very interested in the guidance aspect of money and it seemed we were rapidly being led to purchase the *Maori.*"

2. If Cunningham had not taken this time to be alone with God, He might not have discovered their mistake and things would have been even worse.

///

We should heed the sense of needing to spend time with God in prayer.

///

3. "Suddenly the words of chapter 12, verses 26 and 27 leaped off the page. *'Yet once more I will shake not only the earth, but also the heaven... that those things which cannot be shaken may remain'*... The words on that page of Hebrews had had such power in them! Maybe they did mean the ship! For the rest of my week of prayer, I struggled with this apparent warning-guidance, but nothing became clear."

   God uses Scripture to give guidance—in this case a warning.

4. "We had good experience hearing God when we were all together." Joining with others in prayer to discern God's will can be very helpful.

5. God used a "mental picture" to expose a sinful attitude that needed to be dealt with.

6. "Oh, God! Forgive me! I have gotten my eyes on the ship You're giving us and have taken them off You!...

   "I cried a long time and felt that God had heard and forgiven me. But I knew my attitude wasn't the only one which needed correcting ... We had to do some serious business with the Lord before we thought about anything else."

///

When God points out an area of sin, we need to deal
with it right away. Unrepented sin can act as a
barrier to hearing God's voice.

///

7. "Was it my imagination, or did Kalafi seem less lighthearted than I remembered? I dismissed my first impressions."

   The inner knowing can come in the form of an intuition.

8. A review of ways God had spoken: "Yes, God had told us to get a ship, and repeatedly He had confirmed His guidance, using all the ways we had learned for hearing His voice. He used the Wise Men Principle; He used Scriptures which He seemed to lift off the pages for us; He used provision of money and people, and that inner conviction—but we had failed in the *way* we had carried out His guidance. We had subtly turned from the Giver to the gift."

a. This "inner conviction" is an inner knowing of what to do.

b. We should carry out God's guidance with an attitude that honors Him. It is essential to give the Lord honor and glory. Don't give greater honor to a tool of God's—like a person, curriculum, a ministry, or "a ship"—than you give to God. We want people to be drawn to God, not to us or to our church or ministry.

9. *Caution:* As we learn how to better follow the inner knowing, pride can easily creep in. We need to ask God to show us the inner motives of our hearts. As He reveals any prideful thoughts of being "more spiritual," we need to repent and ask for God's mercy and forgiveness.

10. "Through some instinct of the spirit, we knew He had walked into that bare conference room on the second floor of a hostel outside Osaka. He removed all the guilt. We were clean, forgiven."

Again we see the inner knowing as a "knowing that you know" something.

11. Once more the Lord used Scripture to reveal what He was doing. He used the story of Lazarus and how God was more glorified by resurrecting Lazarus than by healing him.

12. "After we hung up I prayed by myself to make sure, but the truth only grew larger in my mind."

///

When getting guidance from God through another person,
we should go to God and ask Him directly if what was
heard was from Him. God can confirm what is spoken
through another person by giving us an inner
knowing that what was said is true.

///

13. "All I knew was that ever since the day, four weeks
ago, when I read in Hebrews that God was going to
shake what could be shaken, not one dollar had come
in for the ship... Suddenly the flow had been turned
off and only God could have done it."

Financial provision, or lack of it, can be useful in
guidance.

B. Chapter 15

1. "The Three Steps to Hearing God... First, we took
Christ's authority to silence the enemy. Second,
we asked the Lord to clear from our minds any
presumptions and preconceived ideas. Third, we
waited... believing He would speak in the way and in
the time which He chose."

2. "People would 'hear' a Scripture reference in their
minds, without knowing what the verse said. The key,
we were taught there, was yieldedness to Jesus. We
weren't playing some kind of game, pulling a reference
out of the air; we were waiting, listening, focusing our
minds on Jesus alone."

3. God can place thoughts, words or mental pictures in
our minds as we seek His guidance and wait on Him to
speak to us in any way He chooses.

4. God confirmed what He had spoken by telling the students the exact same things.

5. "I explained what had happened, including the grieving Jesus and the Osaka confessions of our sins, especially our pride. I told him how confession opened the door to God's guidance again...." "I consider my money well invested, Loren! God has used it to get your organization humbled before Him. I expect you to move ahead with a special power now."

   Humility allows us to hear God more clearly and to be of greater use to Him.

6. God communicated the need to move on by allowing Cunningham to suddenly feel like he wasn't "home" in Switzerland and to have a sense of discontentment.

7. "It was a strange time for someone interested in guidance because although I was clearly being led *away* from one area, I was not as clearly being led *to* another."

   God usually leads us *to* a new place before He leads us *from* the old place.

8. "Sometimes ... we momentarily lose our axeheads— our best cutting-edge tool for ministry, the clear voice of God. It helps to go back to the place where we last knew we had heard the sharp edge of God's voice."

C. Points 3, 4 and 5

1. Point 3—"Confess any unforgiven sin. A clean heart is necessary if you want to hear God."

2. Point 4—"The key question is: *Have you obeyed the last thing God told you to do?*"

3. Point 5—Get your own leading from God. Others may confirm it.

IV. Supporting Principles From Scripture — Acts 16:1–15
   ## Acts 20:13–38
   ## Acts 21:1–16

A. Acts 16:1–15

1. It is important to recognize the context in which Paul and his companions heard the Lord so clearly.

   They were traveling from town to town delivering the decisions reached by the apostles and elders in Jerusalem for the churches to obey. The believers were benefited greatly by their ministry (**verses 4–5**).

   They were also preaching the Gospel as they traveled and were directed to preach specifically in Macedonia (**verse 10**).

///

God will speak to us as we are faithful in ministering to others and sharing what we know about Jesus.

///

2. Their attitudes were that of obedience and desire to do all that would further the spread of the good news about Christ. Timothy submitted to circumcision in order to eliminate the barrier his Greek heritage

might create. Paul took on the personal discipling of Timothy, a teenager (**verse 3**).

As our hearts are obedient and willing to give up our personal agendas, God will be able to use us to do His work, and He will communicate to us how best to do that.

3. In **verse 6** they were **"kept by the Holy Spirit from preaching the word in the province of Asia."**

   How did the Holy Spirit forbid them from going there?

   If it had been through a word from a prophet or through a vision, it would probably say so in the text. God could have given them this guidance through an inner knowing.

4. In **verse 7** it says that they tried to enter Bithynia and that **"the Spirit of Jesus would not allow them to."** This could be an example of an inner knowing in the form of a sudden uneasiness. So, Paul and his companions did not enter Bithynia. Notice they obediently followed the Spirit's leading even though they did not know exactly where to go.

It is essential to know what God does *not* want us to do and where he does *not* want us to go. We can waste a lot of time and energy doing something good that might not be what God wants us to do, and we will not see the optimum results of our effort.

5. In **verse 9** the Lord spoke to Paul through a vision that directed them to go to Macedonia. The Lord directed them to where the harvest was ripe, where He knew people were ready to hear the Gospel and believe.

6. They traveled to Philippi, and on the Sabbath they went to the river where they expected to find a place of prayer. In cities where there was no synagogue, Jews often gathered in locations along a sea or river.

7. It was there that they met Lydia, who became the first convert in Macedonia. The church at Philippi was started because of their obedience to the Holy Spirit's guidance.

8. Lydia was **"a dealer in purple cloth from the city of Thyatira..." verse 14**.

   a. This province in Asia Minor was well-known for their beautiful purple garments, the dye for which came from a shellfish. This cloth was very expensive and Lydia was most likely very wealthy.

   b. She was **"a worshiper of God" verse 14**. Like the Cornelius of **Acts 10**, Lydia believed in the true God and followed the Jews' moral teaching.

   c. **"The Lord opened her heart to respond to Paul's message" verse 14.**

      Open is translated from a Greek word meaning to open freely the ears, the eyes, the heart; to open one's faculty to learning and understanding.[5]

      Lydia's heart was teachable.

9. Paul and his companions probably had an inner knowing in the form of a peace for them to judge that it was right for them to stay at Lydia's house as she had requested.

B. Acts 20:13–38

1. In this passage we learn that Paul had been determined to arrive in Jerusalem by the day of Pentecost. On his way there he sent for the elders of the church at Ephesus. These verses indicate Paul's recognition of and cooperation with the leadership of a church. His speech modeled for these leaders the attitudes an elder should have (**verses 17–21**).

2. **"I served the Lord with great humility and with tears, although I was severely tested by the plots of the Jews" Acts 20:19.**

//

Contrary to some teaching, the way of a Christian is not always easy. If circumstances are bad, it doesn't necessarily mean that you are out of God's will.

//

3. **Verse 22** shows that Paul was strongly directed by the Holy Spirit to go to Jerusalem, most likely through an inner knowing.

   The Living Bible reads, **"And now I am going to Jerusalem, drawn there irresistibly by the Holy Spirit, not knowing what awaits me...."** The footnote on **verse 22** adds **"by an inner compulsion,"** further indicating an inner knowing.

4. **Verse 23** reads, **"I only know that in every city the Holy Spirit warns me that prison and hardships are facing me."**

   If the Holy Spirit warned Paul using words, this verse is an example of the inner voice, which will be discussed more in the next lesson.

5. **Verse 24** shows Paul's intention to never give up. He was focused on completing the task God had given him. *The International Bible Commentary* includes the following:

   > This journey was not a "mistake," since a Spirit-empowered apostle had received instructions from his Lord about the matter, while the messages through the prophets rightly stressed the danger involved. This is what compelled by the Spirit must mean so that the prison and hardships predicted could not turn him from his course which must be accomplished, irrespective of personal considerations, since his life was not precious to himself but only as a means of serving the Lord.[6]

   We, too, need to keep our focus on what we know God has told us to do, despite the hardships.

6. **"Now I know that none of you ... will ever see me again" Acts 20:25.** *The NIV Study Bible* states that Paul misunderstood the Holy Spirit; he apparently did revisit Ephesus.[7]

   This was not a message from God, but what Paul had anticipated on his own. As it sometimes happens, we can be mistaken about the timing of the events that God has told us will happen.

7. In **verse 28** one of the roles of the Holy Spirit is revealed. He calls certain believers to be overseers of the flock. He is the Father's executive director over all the church, appointing this believer here and another believer there.

   An *overseer,* in Greek, *episkopos* (ep-is´-kop-os), is a superintendent in charge of a church; a bishop.[8] Paul reminded them that they were made **"bishops and guardians, to shepherd (tend and feed and guide) the church of the Lord..." Acts 20:28 AMP**.

   These overseers were to be on their guard against those who would distort the truth in order to draw some disciples to themselves and away from the truth. Paul, by his example and words of instruction, encouraged the overseers to do their God-given job.

///

We are all appointed by God to do certain things,
and it is our responsibility to ask God what they are
and to be faithful to do them.

///

C. Acts 21:1–16

1. When Paul and his friends met with the disciples of Tyre, the Holy Spirit warned the believers there about the suffering that Paul would face in Jerusalem. They drew the conclusion that Paul should not go there (**verse 4**).

2. In Caesarea, a prophet named Agabus foretold Paul's future imprisonment (**verse 11**). The tying of his hands

and feet imitated the symbolic acts of Old Testament prophets. This was the same Agabus in **Acts 11:27–29** who had predicted the famine in Jerusalem 15 years earlier.

3. The Holy Spirit certainly had sufficiently warned Paul ahead of time about the suffering ahead. Paul chose to finish the job given to him by God. He said, **"I am ready not only to be bound, but also to die in Jerusalem for the name of the Lord Jesus." "I am ready"** is equivalent to saying, "I hold myself in readiness" and it speaks of the drive in Paul to accomplish the task set out for him.

   Paul was ready because his daily communication with God had given the Lord the time necessary to prepare Paul. God's kindness is evident here as He didn't ask Paul to do anything he wasn't prepared to do.

4. The Holy Spirit gave Paul his own choice. The choice he made to go to Jerusalem was just like the decision Jesus made. **"As the time approached for him to be taken up to heaven, Jesus resolutely set out for Jerusalem" Luke 9:51**. Both were facing certain death; both had counted the cost and had decided that it was worth the eternal rewards.

5. **"Let us fix our eyes on Jesus, the author and perfecter of our faith, who for the joy set before him endured the cross, scorning its shame, and sat down at the right hand of the throne of God" Hebrews 12:2**.

   The writer of **Hebrews** encourages us to follow Jesus, knowing that we, too, will receive heavenly rewards.

V. Discussion of the Assigned Articles

ASK CLASS MEMBERS TO SHARE WHAT POINTS
IMPACTED THEM THE MOST FROM EACH ARTICLE.

VI. Next Week's Assignment

A. REVIEW NEXT WEEK'S ASSIGNMENT ON THE
COURSE OUTLINE.

B. REVIEW THE MAIN PRINCIPLE FOR NEXT
WEEK'S CLASS

C. ASK PARTICIPANTS TO LOOK IN THE BOOK
AND SCRIPTURE ASSIGNMENTS FOR:
1) PRINCIPLES OF GUIDANCE, AND
2) EXAMPLES OF THE INNER VOICE.

D. DESCRIBE THE INNER VOICE SO THAT THEY
KNOW WHAT TO LOOK FOR.

  1. The inner voice is quiet guidance using words. This
  still, small voice is the gentle whisper of the Holy
  Spirit in your spirit.

  2. Recall the example of the inner voice from Lesson 2.
  This was the incident in which the Lord softly told
  Craig that he would get hit by the ball in that night's
  softball game.

E. ASSIGN DISCUSSION LEADERS FOR LESSON 10
EITHER NOW OR NEXT WEEK: ONE FOR THE
SCRIPTURES, AND ANOTHER TO LEAD THE
BOOK AND ARTICLE DISCUSSIONS.

F. ASK PARTICIPANTS TO PRAY FOR NEXT WEEK'S DISCUSSION LEADERS DURING THE WEEK AND BE READY TO PRAY FOR THEM IN CLASS. ENCOURAGE THEM TO ASK GOD FOR SCRIPTURES OR WORDS OF ENCOURAGEMENT OR EXHORTATION FOR THEM.

VII. Ministry Time

A. AS FACILITATOR, YOU NEED TO GUIDE THE MINISTRY TIME. REFER TO THE CLASS FORMAT SECTION OF THE *FACILITATOR TRAININ STUDY GUIDE* AND READ THE "MINISTRY TIME" SECTION. (Note: The *Facilitator Training Study Guide* is the booklet you received during Facilitator Training.)

B. BE SURE TO PRAY FOR THIS WEEK'S DISCUSSION LEADERS. ENCOURAGE PARTICIPANTS TO SHARE ANY SCRIPTURES OR WORDS OF ENCOURAGEMENT THAT THE LORD GAVE FOR THESE LEADERS.

C. NOTE: THE MINISTRY EMPHASIS HAS NOW SHIFTED TO THE WEEKLY DISCUSSION LEADERS. ANY OTHER PERSONAL MINISTRY SHOULD NOW BE ADDRESSED AFTER CLASS UNLESS THE HOLY SPIRIT STRONGLY DIRECTS YOU OTHERWISE.

D. AT THE BEGINNING OF THE MINISTRY TIME YOU MAY WANT TO REMIND PARTICIPANTS:

As we minister to each other, we need to recognize that we are all fine-tuning our hearing of God's voice. We may not hear clearly all the time, so we need to carefully weigh any word of prophecy a class member gives us. The following is a helpful guideline:

If it doesn't make sense, put it on the shelf. If it contradicts what God has told you, let it drop. If your spirit confirms it, make a note of it in your journal and watch God bring it about.

E. ENCOURAGE HANDS-ON MINISTRY BY CLASS MEMBERS. ALLOW THE GIFTS OF THE SPIRIT TO MANIFEST IN DIFFERENT PEOPLE.

F. BE CAREFUL THAT ONE PERSON DOES NOT DOMINATE THE MINISTERING.

G. CLOSE WITH PRAYER.

LESSON 9

DIFFERENT WAYS GOD SPEAKS — INNER VOICE

MAIN PRINCIPLE

God can communicate with us through the inner voice, which is quiet guidance with words. This still, small voice is the gentle whisper of the Holy Spirit in our spirit.

LESSON 9

Different Ways God Speaks — Inner Voice

I. Let's Get Started!

A. WELCOME THE CLASS AND ENCOURAGE PARTICIPANTS TO SHARE WHAT GOD HAS BEEN DOING IN THEIR LIVES THIS PAST WEEK.

B. OPEN WITH PRAYER.

C. WORSHIP THE LORD.

D. POINT OUT TO THE CLASS THAT ZOE MINISTRIES IS A NONPROFIT ORGANIZATION THAT DEPENDS ON DONATIONS TO ACCOMPLISH THE TASK OF TRAINING AND EQUIPPING PEOPLE TO HEAR, KNOW AND FOLLOW GOD'S VOICE. COURSE FEES GO TOWARDS TRANSLATION, FORMATTING AND PUBLISHING COSTS. ASK THEM TO PRAYERFULLY CONSIDER SUPPORTING ZOE. DIRECT THEM TO THE DONATION FORM IN LESSON 9 OF THE STUDY GUIDE.

E. READ, OR HAVE SOMEONE READ, THE MAIN PRINCIPLE FOR TODAY'S LESSON.

II. Definition of the Inner Voice

The *inner voice* is a still, small voice using words. It is the Holy Spirit's gentle whisper in your spirit.

III. Supporting Principles — Cunningham — Chapters 16–18 and Points 6, 7 and 8

What examples of the inner voice did you find in these chapters? What principles of guidance are found in these chapters?

FOLLOWING ARE SOME SUGGESTED QUOTES FROM THE BOOK. THE HOLY SPIRIT MAY GUIDE YOU TO SOME OTHERS THAT ARE IMPORTANT FOR YOUR CLASS TO DISCUSS.

A. Chapter 16

1. "Regularly we ought to check our progress against our original mandates. My calling was clear: To preach the twin character of the Gospel. Through Jesus Christ it is possible to love God with all our hearts and to love our neighbors as ourselves."

///

As we compare our current life with our original calling, God can give us more insight on what He wants us to do.

///

2. "One of the principles we use in seeking guidance is *ongoing confirmation*, similar to the road signs you would look for on an unfamiliar highway." The example here is God telling Dr. Malmstadt that He was going to give YWAM a university and that Malmstadt was to be a part of it.

3. As the Cunninghams tried to find Tapu, God guided them by impressions for which direction to go (the inner knowing). God also guided them through the inner voice: "Then the Holy Spirit's voice spoke into my mind. *Stop here.*"

4. "Suddenly God spoke to him. Kalafi could hear Him with his natural ears, and he began sweating all over. 'Kalafi,' the Lord said tenderly, 'living the Christian life is difficult. There is only one thing harder—that's not being a Christian. The price that you pay to follow Me is far less than the price you'll have to pay not to follow Me.'"

This is an example of the authoritative voice of the Holy Spirit, which will be discussed in Lesson 10.

5. "Then one of the more intriguing forms of guidance began to take place. Kalafi's landscaping business went sour ... Kalafi finally got the message from the broken down bulldozers and gave up his business; he and Leda were now living on whatever God provided."

God can use circumstances to guide us.

6. Evidence of God's mercy: "If being perfectly at the heart of His will were the criterion for ministry, how many of us would qualify? Fortunately, even when we fail, God does not take back His gifts and callings."

B. Chapter 17

1. God provided quite a bit of ongoing confirmation regarding the ship, so that Cunningham would not give up on it.

   a. Don found the *Victoria*, a *white* ship.

   b. Mr. Ainsworth had a vision of a ship moving through the Pacific leaving revival in its wake.

- When Mr. Ainsworth asked God what he was supposed to do with the vision, "The Lord said, 'Go to Hawaii.'" This an example of the inner voice.

- "Before he left, a friend handed him a piece of paper saying, 'This man may help you. He lives in Hawaii.'"

c. An intercessor wrote, "The Lord told me you and Loren are giving birth to twins. Not literally, I'm sure. I believe the twins are *ministries*. One is the ship. I'm not sure what the other one is...."

This is another example of the inner voice.

d. "We had seen before, at times of great turning points, that it helps to ask ourselves, 'How much of the supernatural is there in the guidance we are receiving?' We had not been asking for signs, nor seeking the spectacular, but signs and spectacular coincidences had been occurring one after another. It seemed spiritual foolishness not to pay attention! God was probably saying, 'This is the way, walk in it.'"

e. "One of the most trustworthy tests for valid guidance is this: Does it bring the people who are involved one step closer to freedom and maturity in the Lord? If this is not so, the guidance is probably suspect. If it is so, the direction is probably from God. In this particular instance, Don Stephens was the principal person being released."

2. "He and I now spent hours lying on the blue carpet of our apartment, praying and planning and brainstorming."

   Prayerful discussion with mature Christians offers God an opportunity to give us ideas and guidance.

3. Danger areas in guidance

   a. "Divine guidance is so heady, so spectacular, that there is the risk of glory attaching itself to the work rather than to the Lord."

   b. "When God guides us, He is taking a risk, too. If we make the wrong choices we can end up not only robbing Him of His *glory*, but of His rightful *first attention*."

      The example here was when Cunningham made the wrong choice of not going directly to the World Cup Soccer Games as God had directed him. Instead, he looked into an offer of funding for God's tool, the university. We need to give God our first attention by keeping in mind what He has told us to do and not letting other good ideas prevent us from obeying Him.

4. *"Guidance is first of all a relationship with the Guide."*
   "The first goal of guidance is to lead us into a closer relationship with Jesus. All other goals should be subservient to that. We have to be especially watchful when He is leading us toward tools, such as a ship or a university. There is nothing wrong with tools. But it's a sad day if the tools ever supersede the Lord Himself."

C. Chapter 18

1. "One of the problems with being led by the Lord is keeping perspective. As divine guidance begins to unfold, it always seems to come with hard, gritty work. Gone is the thrill of the original leading. Ahead, still, is the excitement of seeing the fruit of this same leading. All that's left in between is mind-numbing, muscle-straining labor."

2. "We prayed over these problems, putting the Perspective Principle to work by recalling both the original vision and the future potential of a ship as an evangelistic and mercy ministry tool. We would need this to carry us through the long hard months ahead."

D. Points 6, 7 and 8

1. Point 6—"Don't talk about your guidance until God gives you permission to do so." DISCUSS THE FOUR PITFALLS OF GUIDANCE.

2. Point 7—The Wise Men Principle: "God will often use two or more spiritually sensitive people to *confirm* what He is telling you (**2 Cor. 13:1**)."

3. Point 8—Beware of counterfeit guidance. "The guidance of the Holy Spirit leads you closer to Jesus and into true freedom. Satan's guidance leads you away from God into bondage."

IV. Supporting Principles From Scripture — Acts 4:32 through Acts 5:16

The passages preceding **Acts 5:1–16** set the stage for the story of Ananias and Sapphira. In these verses we see the amazing work of the Holy Spirit, who brought about the unity, love, generosity, grace and power exhibited by the early church. It is in this context that Ananias and Sapphira bring their gift to the apostles and that Peter receives guidance from the Lord.

A. Background—Acts 4:23–31
In this prayer meeting we see amazing unity among the believers.

1. In the *King James Version* **verse 24** reads, **"they raised their voice to God with one accord...."** This phrase, *one accord*, is defined as together, unanimously, with one mind.[1]

2. They had unity because they shared and worked toward a common goal. The goal they shared was to bring people to a saving faith in the resurrected Jesus. They prayed for boldness to speak out the good news about Him (**verse 29**).

3. Their unity came from a common understanding of the work of the Trinity. Their prayer in **verses 29–30** and its outcome in **verse 31** show the work of the Trinity as the believers prayed to *God the Father* to use them to do signs and wonders through the name of His servant *Jesus* in the power of the *Holy Spirit*.

B. Acts 4:32–37

1. **Verse 32** further testifies to their unity: **"All the believers were one in heart and mind."**

2. They *loved* God and one another and showed it by sharing what they had with those in need (**verse 32**). Certainly their gratitude to God for what He had done for them motivated them to share with others. Several wealthy believers sold property and gave the proceeds to the apostles to distribute to those in need (**verses 34–37**). God's love enabled this crossing of socioeconomic boundaries. Their *generosity* must have been a wonderful witness to the love of God.

3. Their willingness to live in unity and love allowed God to give them His *power* and *grace*.

   a. God worked in and through them with power. *Power* in **verse 33** comes from the Greek word *dunamis* (doo´-nam-is), meaning energy, might, great force, ability or strength.[2] The apostles preached with power, and their words were supported by miraculous signs and wonders (**Acts 4:22, 30, 33**).

   b. Their prayers released God's power. **Verse 31** reads, **"After they prayed, the place where they were meeting was shaken. And they were all filled with the Holy Spirit and spoke the word of God boldly."**

   c. **"Much grace was upon them all"** verse 33. *Grace* means favor, gift, benefit, joy and liberality coming from God.[3] They *all* experienced this unmerited favor of God.

//

If we are willing to live in unity and love with other believers, God can give us this same power and grace. We can't do this on our own. We need to ask God to give us His love for others and we need to choose to act lovingly.

//

C. Acts 5:1–16

1. In **Acts 5:1–2** we read of Ananias' and Sapphira's deception and hypocrisy. They jointly decided to deceive the church by selling a piece of property and giving part of the proceeds to the apostles, but claiming that they were giving all of the proceeds. Ananias and Sapphira didn't appear to operate with the grace, power and unity that God made available to believers.

2. Because the hatred and persecution toward Christians was so great, no one would claim to believe in Jesus unless they had a real salvation experience.[4] So we must assume that Ananias and Sapphira were believers despite their behavior.

3. In **verses 3–4** we see that Peter received information from God about what Ananias and Sapphira had done. The Holy Spirit probably spoke to Peter through an *inner voice.*

   a. In **verse 3** Peter said, **"Ananias, how is it that Satan has so filled your heart that you have lied to the Holy Spirit...?"**

   Can Satan fill a Christian's spirit?

   No. Remember that the word *heart* can represent either the spirit or the soul; in this case it refers to the soul. Once you have accepted Christ, the

Holy Spirit dwells in your spirit and Satan cannot fill it. However, your soul—your mind, will and emotions—can definitely be influenced by the enemy. This was the case with Ananias and Sapphira. Satan tempted them, they yielded to that temptation and allowed Satan to influence their mind, will and emotions. They chose to lie to the other believers and to God.

b. We also need to have discernment like Peter did. We normally look at the outward appearance and behavior of someone, while God looks at his heart (**1 Samuel 16:7**). God can tell us when people are not how they appear.

4. In **verse 4b** Peter said, **"What made you think of such a thing?"** Satan was able to tempt Ananias and Sapphira to lie because they wanted to win the approval of the other Christians. They didn't want to give all the money away, which was fine, but they chose to not be honest about it. Their deception was deliberate, and stemmed from wanting to look good in the eyes of others. They were more concerned with winning the approval of men than having the approval of God. Sapphira didn't confess and repent even when given the chance (**verse 8**).

5. There was no excuse for Ananias and Sapphira. They had personally experienced God's saving grace; they had seen His power producing good things in those around them. The Holy Spirit had probably tried to bring them to repentance by allowing them to see His kindness as He worked in their life (**Romans 2:4**). Yet they had hardened their hearts, and they chose to lie.

6. The worst part of their sin seems to have been that they lied to God, the Holy Spirit (**verses 3, 4, 9**). They thought they could fool the Holy Spirit.

7. *The NIV Study Bible* has a helpful footnote to **verse 9** on testing the Spirit of the Lord.

> If no dire consequences had followed this act of sin, the results among the believers would have been serious when the deceit became known. Not only would dishonesty appear profitable, but the conclusion that the Spirit could be deceived would follow. It was important to set the course properly at the outset in order to leave no doubt that God will not tolerate such hypocrisy and deceit.[5]

We need to take this lesson to heart as well.

a. Are we stuck in habitual sin, thinking we can hide it from God or that it doesn't matter?

b. Are we more concerned with winning the approval of other people than we are of winning God's approval?

8. The phrase **"great fear seized"** is found twice in this passage in reference to the reaction in people who heard of the deaths of Ananias and Sapphira (**verses 5** and **11**). This is not a negative kind of fear, but a positive kind.

a. Fear of the Lord involves holding God in awe and respect. It includes an awareness of God's omnipresence and omniscience, and a desire to please Him only and always because of who He is. Fear of the Lord is viewing sin as God does—with hatred.[6]

b. We see in **verses 12–16** the results of the **"great fear that seized the whole church and all who heard about these events."** The results included:

- Signs and wonders were performed through the apostles.

- Many were healed of diseases and freed from evil spirits.

- The believers were held in awe and were highly regarded by the people.

- Many more came to faith in Jesus.

9. These results came about because Peter heeded the inner voice, which told him what Ananias and Sapphira had done.

V. Discussion of the Assigned Articles

ASK CLASS MEMBERS TO SHARE WHAT POINTS IMPACTED THEM MOST FROM EACH ARTICLE.

VI. Next Week's Assignment

A. REVIEW NEXT WEEK'S ASSIGNMENT ON THE COURSE OUTLINE.

B. REVIEW THE MAIN PRINCIPLE FOR NEXT WEEK'S LESSON.

C. ASK PARTICIPANTS TO LOOK AT THE BOOK
AND SCRIPTURE READING ASSIGNMENTS FOR:
1) PRINCIPLES OF GUIDANCE, AND
2) EXAMPLES OF THE AUTHORITATIVE VOICE.

D. DESCRIBE THE AUTHORITATIVE VOICE SO
THAT THEY KNOW WHAT TO LOOK FOR.

1. The authoritative voice of the Holy Spirit is so loud
   that you think you are hearing it with your ears and
   that others can hear it also.

2. REMIND THE CLASS OF THE EXAMPLE OF
   THE AUTHORITATIVE VOICE FROM LESSON 2.
   An example was when Craig was playing in a worship
   band and watching a family receive prayer. He heard the
   Lord say loudly, "There she is! That is the girl you are
   going to marry."

E. ASK ONE CLASS MEMBER TO PREPARE TO LEAD
THE SCRIPTURE DISCUSSION AND ANOTHER
TO LEAD THE BOOK AND ASSIGNED ARTICLE
DISCUSSION FOR LESSON 11, EITHER NOW OR
NEXT WEEK.

F. REMIND PARTICIPANTS TO PRAY FOR NEXT
WEEK'S DISCUSSION LEADERS DURING THE
WEEK AND BE READY TO PRAY FOR THEM IN
CLASS. ENCOURAGE THEM TO ASK GOD FOR
SCRIPTURES OR WORDS OF ENCOURAGEMENT
OR EXHORTATION FOR THEM.

VII. Ministry

A. AS FACILITATOR, YOU NEED TO GUIDE THE MINISTRY TIME. REFER TO THE CLASS FORMAT SECTION OF THE *FACILITATOR TRAINING STUDY GUIDE* AND READ THE "MINISTRY TIME" SECTION. (Note: The *Facilitator Traning Study Guide* is the booklet you received during Facilitator Training.)

B. BE SURE TO PRAY FOR THIS WEEK'S DISCUSSION LEADERS. ENCOURAGE PARTICIPANTS TO SHARE ANY SCRIPTURES OR WORDS OF ENCOURAGEMENT THAT THE LORD GAVE FOR THESE LEADERS.

C. NOTE: THE MINISTRY EMPHASIS HAS NOW SHIFTED TO THE WEEKLY DISCUSSION LEADERS. ANY OTHER PERSONAL MINISTRY SHOULD NOW BE ADDRESSED AFTER CLASS UNLESS THE HOLY SPIRIT STRONGLY DIRECTS YOU OTHERWISE.

D. AT THE BEGINNING OF THE MINISTRY TIME YOU MAY WANT TO REMIND PARTICIPANTS:

As we minister to each other, we need to recognize that we are all fine-tuning our hearing of God's voice. We may not hear clearly all the time, so we need to carefully weigh any word of prophecy a class member gives us. The following is a helpful guideline:

If it doesn't make sense, put it on the shelf. If it contradicts what God has told you, let it drop. If your spirit confirms it, make a note of it in your journal and watch God bring it about.

E. ENCOURAGE HANDS-ON MINISTRY BY CLASS MEMBERS. ALLOW THE GIFTS OF THE SPIRIT TO MANIFEST IN DIFFERENT PEOPLE.

F. BE CAREFUL THAT ONE PERSON DOES NOT DOMINATE THE MINISTERING.

G. CLOSE WITH PRAYER.

LESSON 10

DIFFERENT WAYS GOD SPEAKS – AUTHORITATIVE VOICE OF THE HOLY SPIRIT

MAIN PRINCIPLE

The Holy Spirit can speak to believers with words that seem to us to be audible to those around us. What He says will never contradict Scripture.

LESSON 10

Different Ways God Speaks — Authoritative Voice

I. Let's Get Started!

A. WELCOME THE CLASS AND ENCOURAGE PARTICIPANTS TO SHARE WHAT GOD HAS BEEN DOING IN THEIR LIVES THIS PAST WEEK.

B. OPEN WITH PRAYER.

C. WORSHIP THE LORD.

D. READ, OR HAVE SOMEONE READ, THE MAIN PRINCIPLE FOR TODAY'S LESSON.

II. Definition of the Authoritative Voice of the Holy Spirit

The *authoritative voice* is like the inner voice, in that you hear the guidance in the form of words. However, the authoritative voice is so loud that you may think you are hearing it with your ears and that others can hear it also.

When God speaks through the authoritative voice, it is usually for protection, direction or strong instruction.

III. Supporting Principles — Cunningham — Chapters 19 and 20 and Points 9 and 10

What examples of the authoritative voice did you find in these chapters? What principles of guidance are found in these chapters?

FOLLOWING ARE SOME SUGGESTED QUOTES FROM THE BOOK. THE HOLY SPIRIT MAY GUIDE YOU TO SOME OTHERS THAT ARE IMPORTANT FOR YOUR CLASS TO DISCUSS.

A. Chapter 19

1. "Don became intrigued by the link between prayer and fasting, guidance, and a good harvest. Jesus, after all, began His incredibly fruitful ministry after the wilderness fast."

2. God supernaturally caused fish to jump on shore, and thereby communicated His intention to bless the ministry of the *Anastasis*.

3. God communicated the correct timing of the establishment of the twin ministries of the university and the ship by having an obstetrician give a warning. "He repeated again and again: We must see the second twin, U of N, born shortly or both the mother—YWAM—and the second twin would die."

B. Chapter 20

1. "Along the way, I had stumblingly learned how to hear His voice, and even more stumblingly, was learning to obey."

We can learn from the author's and our own mistakes and successes. As we become more sensitive to God's voice and more obedient to do what He says, we will see God's power released in our ministries.

2. "Put your dreams on the altar. They will be resurrected into something even grander."

3. "This is what hearing God is all about... Getting to know Him better."

C. Points 9 and 10

1. Point 9—"Opposition from man is sometimes guidance from God ... The important thing here, again, is *yieldedness* to the Lord."

2. Point 10—"The more you seek to hear God's voice in detail, the more effective you will be in your own calling. Guidance is ... serious business where we learn *what* God wants us to do in ministry and *how* He wants us to do it."

IV. Supporting Principles From Scripture — 1 Samuel 1, 2 and 3

A. 1 Samuel 1

1. Hannah is the main character in this chapter. Her name means graciousness.[1] She was the favored wife of Elkanah. He had a precious love for her even though she was unable to bear him children (**verses 5, 8**).

2. In **verses 2–8** we read of Hannah's plight. Her inability to have children was a cause of great distress for her.

   a. Not only was she missing the joy of having children, but she had to endure the scorn and provocation of her husband's other wife, Peninnah.

   b. In her culture, barrenness could be a sign of God's disapproval. In **verse 6** it says, **"The Lord had closed her womb."** Dake comments on this phrase: "It was customary in those days to attribute all such conditions to God, but in reality they could have been caused by a number of things, as in cases today."[2]

///

Hannah's righteousness may have been questioned by her contemporaries. In actuality, Hannah had a very good understanding of God, and she confidently turned to Him for help. The love her husband showed to her indicates that Hannah had many admirable qualities. It would have been very hard on her to have her righteousness questioned.

///

3. Hannah serves as a good model in regards to prayer.

   a. Although she was greatly distressed over her barrenness, she had not turned away from the Lord. Instead, she looked to Him for help. Hannah did not resort to revenge against Peninnah.

   b. She recognized the covenant-honoring nature of God and made a vow. She vowed that if God would give her a son, she would give him to God as a Nazirite for life. Nazirites were reserved for and dedicated to the Lord for a specified period of time.

This vow called for the Nazirite to refrain from cutting his hair during that time period (**Numbers 6:1–21**).

   c. Hannah was persistent in prayer. **Verse 12** says, **"As she kept on praying...."**

   d. She prayed with honesty and fervency. Hannah was **"pouring out her soul to the Lord."** She honestly told the Lord how she felt and what she was thinking. In deep intercession, Hannah prayed out of her **"great anguish and grief" verses 15–16**.

4. Eli was the priest at this time, as were his grown sons, Hophni and Phinehas.

   a. Eli was obviously not in communication with God regarding Hannah; he accused her of being drunk when she actually was praying to God. This shows how far from God Eli was (**verses 13–14**).

   b. Despite Eli's wrong judgment of Hannah, God still honored Eli's priestly position by inspiring his blessing for her. Eli said, **"Go in peace, and may the God of Israel grant you what you have asked of him" verse 17**.

The word *peace* is *shalom* (shaw-lome´) in Hebrew. It means wholeness, health, safety, soundness, tranquillity, prosperity, rest, harmony, the absence of agitation and discord.[3]

5. Hannah said, **"May your servant find favor in your eyes" verse 18**.

a. The word *favor* comes from the root word *chanan* (khan-an´), which means to be gracious, show mercy or to grant.[4]

b. Hannah believed in Eli's blessing. She appropriated and acted upon it. She **"ate something and her face was no longer downcast" verse 18**. This change in Hannah's attitude and actions indicates that her faith had been strengthened.

6. **Verse 19** says, **"And the Lord remembered her."** This *remember* is the same word that was discussed in Lesson 3 in relation to Noah. "To remember in the Bible is not merely to recall to mind; it is to express concern for someone, to act with loving care for him. When God remembers his people, he does so 'with favor.'"[5] And so God remembered Hannah and enabled her to bear a child.

7. Hannah honored her vow and dedicated Samuel to the Lord. The name *Samuel* sounds like the Hebrew word for "heard of God."[6]

8. Hannah kept Samuel with her until he was weaned **(verse 22)**.

The NIV Study Bible states:

> He would then be two or three years old. There were women engaged in tabernacle service to whose care he might have been committed. It was important that he should be dedicated as soon as possible. The earliest impressions of his boyhood were to be those of the house of the Lord.[7]

B. 1 Samuel 2

1. In this chapter we see the stark contrast between the relationship Eli and his sons had with God versus the relationship Hannah and her son had with God.

   a. Hannah's victory prayer in **verses 1–10** reveals her knowledge of the Lord. She praised God for His mightiness, holiness, omniscience, sovereignty, righteousness and mercy.

   b. Hannah did not pray only when she needed something; she also prayed to express her gratitude and joy in the Lord (**verse 1**).

   c. She prayed prophetically about what God would do in the future (**verses 9–10**). The Lord imparted that prophetic word to her, an ordinary housewife.

   d. Samuel ministered before the Lord (**verse 11**). This was a position of honor; not just anyone was allowed to minister before the Lord.

   e. In contrast, Eli's sons, Hophni and Phinehas, are described in **verse 12** as **"wicked men; they had no regard for the Lord."**

   f. They treated the Lord's offering with contempt, not adhering to the rules for sacrifice, and greedily taking more than their share of the sacrificial meat (**verses 13–17**). **Verse 17 says, "This sin of the young men was very great in the Lord's sight."** They did not walk in the fear of the Lord.

g. Again Samuel is mentioned as ministering before the Lord (**verse 18**). Samuel wore an ephod, which was a priestly garment worn by those who served the Lord in His sanctuary. This is not the special ephod worn by the high priest (**Leviticus 8:7–8**).[8] However, even as a young child, Samuel fulfilled some priestly duties.

h. Every year Hannah would bring a new robe for Samuel to wear (**verse 19**). In doing this, Hannah was keeping Samuel on target for the call on his life. The robe reminded him of the role to which God had called him.

i. **Verse 21b** reads, **"Samuel grew up in the presence of the Lord."**

j. In contrast, Eli's sons committed adultery with the women who served at the entrance to the Tent of Meeting (**verse 22**). They used their position as priests to satisfy their fleshly desires, not to honor God and help the people come closer to Him.

k. They did not repent when Eli rebuked them for their sin and warned them about sinning against the Lord (**verse 25**).

l. In contrast, **verse 26** reads, **"And the boy Samuel continued to grow in stature and in favor with the Lord and with men."** Jesus is described the same way in **Luke 2:52.** (This verse can be made into a prayer for our children by substituting their names for Samuel's.)

///

The contrast is strong between the relationship Samuel had
with God and the relationship Eli's sons had with God.
Samuel and Eli's sons lived in the same environment,
but the condition of their hearts and the choices
they made were very different.

///

    m. In **verses 27–36** a man of God came to Eli with
a word from God in which Eli was confronted
with his sin: **"Why do you scorn my sacrifice
and offering that I prescribed for my dwelling?
Why do you honor your sons more than me by
fattening yourselves on the choice parts of every
offering made by my people Israel?"** verse 29. 1
Samuel 3:13 says Eli failed to restrain his sons.

        Eli's, Hophni's and Phinehas' attitudes and actions
cut them off from fellowship with the Lord. No
wonder the Word of the Lord was rare in their day (**1
Samuel 3:1**)!

2. Are there present-day versions of Eli's sins that
we could be guilty of, which would hamper our
relationship with God?

    a. Do we scorn God's sacrifice and offering of His
Son by failing to tell people about mankind's
sinfulness and Jesus' death to pay the penalty for
our sins?

    b. Do we fail to appropriate the grace that God makes
available to us through taking communion, the
memorial offering of Jesus' sacrifice and blood
covenant?

c. Do we honor our children more than God by not chastening our children about specific areas in their lives because we don't want to face their arguments or don't want to appear different from their friends' parents?

3. The man of God told Eli how the Lord planned to punish Eli's family and to remove them from the priesthood. He also shared God's solution to this problem. God promised to raise up for Himself **"a faithful priest, who will do according to what is in my heart and mind" verse 35**.

In order for anyone to "do according to what is in God's heart and mind," that person would need to know God, recognize His voice and be obedient.

C. 1 Samuel 3

1. **"The boy Samuel ministered before the Lord under Eli" 1 Samuel 3:1.** *The NIV Study Bible* footnote states, "Samuel is now no longer a little child. The Jewish historian Josephus places his age at 12 years; he may have been older."[9]

2. We know this took place before the early morning hours because that was when the large golden lamp stand in the Holy Place became dim or went out[10] (**verse 3**).

3. **Verse 1** says, **"In those days the word of the Lord was rare; there were not many visions."** In **verse 7** it says that Samuel **"did not yet know the Lord: The word of the Lord had not yet been revealed to him."** The word *know* is translated from the Hebrew word *yada* (yaw-dah´). It means to observe with the

eyes, be acquainted with or to know by experience.[11]

Samuel did not recognize the Lord's voice because he had no experience in hearing His voice. Living in those days and with Eli, Samuel didn't have much opportunity to observe others hearing God.

///

It should be encouraging to know that Samuel, who became such a great man of God, started out having no experience in hearing God's voice.

///

4. **Verses 4–8** contain a great example of the authoritative voice of God. The voice Samuel heard seemed so loud that he thought it was Eli calling him.

5. Finally, after Samuel came to him three times, Eli discerned that it was God calling Samuel. He advised Samuel that if the Lord called again, to say, **"Speak, Lord, for your servant is listening" verse 9**.

   This is the receptive attitude towards God that we want to have.

6. Samuel then experienced a vision of God speaking to him (**verses 10–15**). The words God spoke to Samuel about Eli and his family confirmed the earlier prophet's word (**1 Samuel 2:27–36**).

7. Eli must have recognized this because he resigned himself to his fate. He said, **"He is the Lord; let him do what is good in his eyes" verse 18**.

8. Remember that when someone hears the authoritative voice of the Holy Spirit, it is usually for protection,

direction or strong instruction. Eli received strong instruction from the Lord. God let him know that He would no longer tolerate contempt for God's offering. This also served as direction for Samuel.

9. In **verses 19–21** we see Samuel established as a prophet of the Lord.

   a. The Lord was with Samuel as he grew up. The Lord must have trained Samuel to hear His voice since we read that God let none of Samuel's **"words fall to the ground" 1 Samuel 3:19.**

   Looking at the following explanation of this phrase from *Dake's Annotated Reference Bible* may be helpful. Samuel "spoke only as God inspired him, so that every prediction was literally fulfilled. He also gave only sound and divine advice to Israel, so that all his counsels were received as coming from Jehovah."[12]

   b. In **verse 21** we read that God continued to reveal Himself to Samuel as He did in **verse 10**, through the word of the Lord. Samuel then would pass on to the Israelites what God had said to him (**1 Samuel 4:1**). Samuel became a great priest, prophet and judge who loved and honored God.

D. **Closing Teaching**—AT THE END OF THE SCRIPTURE DISCUSSION YOU MAY TEACH THE FOLLOWING MATERIAL.

Like Samuel, we want to say, **"Speak, Lord, your servant is listening."** However, we need to allow God to speak to us in whatever way *He* chooses.

1. We should not specifically seek God's authoritative

voice. Satan can counterfeit audible voices.

2. We should check our motives and ask ourselves if what we think God is saying will bring glory to God, or ourselves.

3. We can ask God to confirm through mature Christians what we have heard.

4. We can look to see what doors God has opened or closed.

5. We should compare what we think God is saying to us with the written Word of God; it should not contradict Scripture.

V. Discussion of the Assigned Articles

ASK CLASS MEMBERS TO SHARE WHAT POINTS IMPACTED THEM THE MOST FROM EACH ARTICLE.

VI. Next Week's Assignment

A. REVIEW NEXT WEEK'S ASSIGNMENT ON THE COURSE OUTLINE.

B. REVIEW THE MAIN PRINCIPLE FOR NEXT WEEK'S LESSON.

C. IF NEEDED, ASSIGN DISCUSSION LEADERS FOR LESSON 11: ONE FOR THE SCRIPTURES AND ANOTHER TO LEAD THE BOOK AND ARTICLE DISCUSSIONS.

YOU DON'T NEED TO ASSIGN DISCUSSION LEADERS FOR LESSON 12. YOU WILL LEAD THE DISCUSSION AND THE BREAKING OF BREAD FOR THAT CLASS.

D. REMIND PARTICIPANTS TO PRAY FOR NEXT WEEK'S DISCUSSION LEADERS DURING THE WEEK AND BE READY TO PRAY FOR THEM IN CLASS. ENCOURAGE THEM TO ASK GOD FOR SCRIPTURES OR WORDS OF ENCOURAGEMENT OR EXHORTATION FOR THEM.

VII. Ministry Time

A. AS FACILITATOR, YOU NEED TO GUIDE THE MINISTRY TIME. REFER TO THE CLASS FORMAT SECTION OF THE *FACILITATOR TRAINING STUDY GUIDE* AND READ THE "MINISTRY TIME" SECTION. (Note: The *Facilitator Training Study Guide* is the booklet you received during Facilitator Training.)

B. BE SURE TO PRAY FOR THIS WEEK'S DISCUSSION LEADERS. ENCOURAGE PARTICIPANTS TO SHARE ANY SCRIPTURES OR WORDS OF ENCOURAGEMENT THAT THE LORD GAVE FOR THESE LEADERS.

C. NOTE: THE MINISTRY EMPHASIS HAS NOW SHIFTED TO THE WEEKLY DISCUSSION LEADERS. ANY OTHER PERSONAL MINISTRY SHOULD NOW BE ADDRESSED AFTER CLASS UNLESS THE HOLY SPIRIT STRONGLY DIRECTS YOU OTHERWISE.

D. AT THE BEGINNING OF THE MINISTRY TIME YOU MAY WANT TO REMIND PARTICIPANTS:

As we minister to each other, we need to recognize that we are all fine-tuning our hearing of God's voice. We may not hear clearly all the time, so we need to carefully weigh any word of prophecy a class member gives us. The following is a helpful guideline:

If it doesn't make sense, put it on the shelf. If it contradicts what God has told you, let it drop. If your spirit confirms it, make a note of it in your journal and watch God bring it about.

E. ENCOURAGE HANDS-ON MINISTRY BY CLASS MEMBERS. ALLOW THE GIFTS OF THE SPIRIT TO MANIFEST IN DIFFERENT PEOPLE.

F. BE CAREFUL THAT ONE PERSON DOES NOT DOMINATE THE MINISTERING.

G. CLOSE WITH PRAYER.

LESSON 11

OTHER MANIFESTATIONS OF THE HOLY SPIRIT

MAIN PRINCIPLE

*God can communicate with us through dreams,
visions and other manifestations
of the Holy Spirit.*

Other Manifestations of the Holy Spirit

I. Let's Get Started!

A. WELCOME THE CLASS AND ENCOURAGE PARTICIPANTS TO SHARE WHAT GOD HAS BEEN DOING IN THEIR LIVES THIS PAST WEEK.

B. OPEN WITH PRAYER.

C. WORSHIP THE LORD.

D. READ, OR HAVE SOMEONE READ, THE MAIN PRINCIPLE FOR TODAY'S LESSON.

II. Supporting Principles — Cunningham — Points 11 and 12 and Review all Points

A. Point 11—"Practice hearing God's voice and it becomes easier." As a young boy, Samuel was not able to recognize God's voice as God called out his name (**1 Samuel 3:4–7**). But by the time the gray-haired Samuel confirmed Saul as king, he was able to call upon the Lord to send thunder and rain on the wheat harvest with confidence, knowing God would do it (**1 Samuel 12:11–18**).

B. Point 12—"Relationship is the most important reason for hearing the voice of the Lord ... We grow to know the Lord better as He speaks to us and, as we listen to Him and obey, we make His heart glad" (**Exodus 33:11; Matthew 7:24–27**).

Moses is an example of how close a relationship we can have with God. **"The Lord would speak to Moses face to face, as a man speaks with his friend" Exodus 33:11a.**

C. Review of All Points

1. What heart attitudes are needed to hear God's voice clearly?

   a. The desire to please God and obey Him (Point 1).

   b. Humbleness and submissiveness to God's lordship (Point 1).

   c. Recognition of your authority over the enemy (Point 1).

   d. Expectancy that your loving Father will answer you (Point 1).

   e. Yieldedness—Allowing God to choose the manner in which He speaks to you (Point 2) and being open to hearing God say something unexpected (Point 9).

   f. A heart free of unconfessed sins (Point 3).

   g. A heart free of pride and presumption (Point 6).

   h. A heart free of rebellion (Point 9).

2. ASK THE CLASS IF THEY HAVE ANY QUESTIONS ABOUT ANY OF THE POINTS.

3. Point 2 lists the ways God may choose to speak to you. They include through His Word, an audible voice, the quiet inner voice, dreams and visions. (The

inner knowing is not mentioned specifically here, but we believe that it is a valid way God speaks to His children.)

a. **Matthew 2** is cited as an example for *dreams*. This chapter includes three dreams God gave Joseph. In the first, an angel told him to escape from Herod and take Mary and Jesus to Egypt. In the second dream, Joseph was told that it was safe to return to Israel. In the third dream, Joseph was warned to move to Nazareth. All these dreams provided protection for Jesus and His parents.

b. Examples of visions include:

Isaiah 6:1—Isaiah had a vision of God on His heavenly throne. He was cleansed and commissioned to go prophesy to the people of Judah.

Revelation 1:12–17—John had a heavenly vision in which he saw someone **"like a son of man"** who gave him a message for the seven churches in Asia.

4. POINT 6 MENTIONS FOUR PITFALLS OF GUIDANCE. UNLESS YOUR CLASS HAS ALREADY DONE SO IN A PREVIOUS LESSON, ASK IF ANYONE CAN SHARE AN EXPERIENCE WHERE THEY TALKED ABOUT GOD'S GUIDANCE WITH OTHERS WITH THE WRONG TIMING OR METHOD.

5. The description of the will of God in Point 10 can be a bit overwhelming, i.e., "The will of God is doing and saying the right thing at the right time...." Remember that guidance is serious business, but that it involves a process that God takes us through over time. As we

gain more experience in guidance we will get better at saying and doing exactly what God has told us.

//

It is worth mentioning again that one key test for true guidance is asking, "Does your leading follow principles of the Bible?" "The Holy Spirit never contradicts the Word of God" (Point 8).

//

III. Supporting Principles From Scripture — Acts 9:1–19
Acts 10:1–48

Note examples of other manifestations of the Holy Spirit. What principles of guidance are found in the assigned reading?

A. Acts 9:1–19

1. **Background**—In **Acts 8:1–3** we read that since the stoning of Stephen, the church at Jerusalem was persecuted. This persecution caused believers to be scattered throughout Judea and Samaria. And, wherever the believers went, they carried the Gospel with them. Persecution of the Body of Christ always brings growth. No wonder the Jewish leaders were bent on destroying the church! Saul actually went from house to house dragging Christian men and women off to prison.

2. **Acts 9:1–19** tells of Saul's conversion. God accomplished this miraculous conversion using several manifestations of the Holy Spirit.

3. It was while Saul was on his way to Damascus to take Christians captive that the Lord got his full attention. Saul and his companions saw a bright light flash around Saul, and Saul fell to the ground (**verses 3–4**).

   a. *Light* in **verse 3** is the same word, *phos* (foce) in Greek, as the light in **1 John 1:5**: **"God is light; in him there is no darkness at all."**[1]

   b. Saul fell to the ground. The presence of God can have this effect at times (**John 18:2–6; Revelation 1:17**).

4. Saul's friends heard a sound, but didn't understand what the Lord was saying to him (**Acts 9:7; 22:9**). Saul **"heard a voice say, 'Saul, why do you persecute me? ... I am Jesus, whom you are persecuting ... Now get up and go into the city, and you will be told what you must do'" Acts 9:4–6.**

///

To the Lord, persecuting His disciples was the same as persecuting Him. We are the body of Christ on earth.

///

5. In **Acts 26:14** Paul tells King Agrippa about his conversion. In this account Jesus said, **"Saul, Saul, why do you persecute me? It is hard for you to kick against the goads."**

   A goad is a long stick with a pointed end. Farmers used it to prod animals to keep them moving. "To kick against the goads" is a Greek proverb that means to **"keep offering vain and perilous resistance" (AMP).** This indicates that Saul had been resisting what God wanted to do. Paul is portrayed as pricked by his conscience over his compliance in Stephen's death and persecution of other believers.[2]

6. **"For three days he was blind, and did not eat or drink anything" verse 9**. What went on in Saul's mind during those three days? He must have been trying to make sense of what had happened to him. He didn't eat, which could have meant that he was fasting to gain spiritual insight, or that he was so emotionally distressed that he couldn't eat. Saul certainly had been humbled and he probably was convicted of sin. He may have considered the direction his life had been going and where it should go now.

7. In **verses 10–16** Ananias had a *vision*.

   a. Ananias was an impeccable witness to the reality of Saul's conversion. He was a disciple and **"was a devout observer of the law and highly respected by all the Jews living there" Acts 22:12**. Ananias' name means: "The Lord is gracious or shows grace."[3]

   Grace can be defined as favor, gift, benefit, joy and liberality coming from God.[4] God's grace, His undeserved favor, was extended to Saul through Ananias.

   b. In this vision the Lord called to Ananias. He recognized the Lord immediately and was ready to serve Him.

   c. The Lord gave Ananias instructions during this vision. In **verses 11–12** Ananias was given *a word of knowledge* that Saul was praying and that Saul had also had a *vision*—Ananias coming to lay hands on him to restore his sight. A word or message of knowledge is one of the manifestations of the Spirit mentioned in **1 Corinthians 12:7–11.**

"The *word of knowledge* is the supernatural revelation to man of some detail of the knowledge of God. It is the impartation of facts and information which are humanly impossible to know ... It may be knowledge of the thoughts of men's hearts ... It may involve men's plans ... or motives ... It may be knowledge of facts of the past, present or future ... It may reveal the whereabouts of men ... or warn of coming danger...."[5]

d. In **verses 13–14** Ananias posed a question to the Lord. These statements about Saul are not so much an expression of Ananias' doubt or fear as they are a request for understanding.

e. The Lord replied with another *word of knowledge* for Ananias in **verses 15** and **16**, telling Ananias facts about the future that he could not humanly know.

f. **"But the Lord said to Ananias, 'Go! This man is my chosen instrument to carry my name before the Gentiles...'" verse 15.** God appointed Saul to carry His name. To *carry* or *bear* means "to raise as a flag; to carry as a banner; support, exalt, and hold upright."[6]

g. God's command to Ananias, **"Go!"** was not meant to scold him but to commission him (**verse 15**). Later in **verse 17**, Ananias said that the Lord Jesus had sent him to Saul. To be *sent* is *apostello* (ap-os-tel´-low) in Greek, which means to appoint someone, to be sent on a mission, to be commissioned as a messenger.[7]

8. So Ananias went to the house of Judas on Straight Street, walked up to Saul and laid hands on him to impart the Holy Spirit to him and to restore his sight.

   a. It might have seemed dangerous to go to that house because there were most likely other Jews there who were antagonistic toward believers. However, strengthened by the Lord's words about what He was doing in Saul's life, Ananias probably decided to trust God and obey Him.

   b. In **verse 17** Ananias said, **"the Lord—Jesus, who appeared to you on the road"** and **Acts 9:27** says that Barnabas **"told them how Saul on his journey had seen the Lord."** *The NIV Study Bible* footnote says, "The Damascus road experience was not merely a vision. The resurrected Christ actually appeared to Saul, and upon this fact Saul based his qualification to be an apostle (**1 Cor. 9:1; 15:8**)."[8]

   c. Ananias was a lay person. **Verse 17** is the first account of the Holy Spirit being imparted through an ordinary believer.

   d. Ananias was given a *gift of healing* for Saul (**1 Corinthians 12:9**). Saul's sight was restored and he was more than ready to be baptized in the name of Jesus.

9. Following are the manifestations of the Holy Spirit included in this passage:

   a. Saul seeing the light from heaven and hearing Jesus' voice

b. Ananias' vision and the words of knowledge about Saul

c. Saul's vision of Ananias coming to lay hands on him

d. The gift of healing for Saul

10. Why was God so generous with all these manifestations of His Spirit?

   a. God used these manifestations of the Spirit to bring Saul to faith in Jesus, so that he could carry Jesus' name **"before the Gentiles and their kings and before the people of Israel" verse 15**.

   b. A purpose of the manifestations of the Holy Spirit is to bring people to a saving faith in Jesus so that they can have fellowship with God.

B. Acts 10:1–48

1. **Overview**—Since Pentecost, the Gospel had been withheld from the Gentiles. Until this point it did not occur to the church that anyone could be saved, unless he was circumcised and kept the law of Moses. In this passage God used several manifestations of the Spirit to bring Cornelius and his Gentile household to faith in Jesus.

2. Even though Cornelius was devout and God-fearing, he still needed to hear the Gospel message. Some people today think that certain behaviors or characteristics will qualify them to go to heaven. This story about Cornelius shows that this is not true.

Things that do not save people include:

a. Being devout, pious or dutiful to religion (**Acts 10:2**)

b. Fearing God—even the demons fear God (**James 2:19**)

c. Giving money to the poor—the Pharisees did this and rejected salvation. One can give all that he has and still be lost (**Ephesians 2:8–9**).

d. Praying often—hypocrites and pagans pray often (**Matthew 6:5**)

e. Being righteous in the eyes of men (**Acts 10:22**)

f. Having a good reputation (**Acts 10:22**)—Saul was well thought of by Jewish leaders while he murdered Christians.

g. Fasting—hypocrites could fast regularly (**Matthew 6:16**)

Peter summed up how anyone can be qualified to go to heaven in **Acts 10:43, "All the prophets testify about him [Jesus] that everyone who believes in him receives forgiveness of sins through his name."**

3. Cornelius' actions indicate that he was seeking God, and God responded by giving him a *vision* of an angel telling him to send for Peter (**verse 3–6**). (This is proof that God is a rewarder of those who diligently seek Him—**Hebrews 11:6**.)

4. God prepared Peter for his encounter with Cornelius (**verses 9–16**). Peter was in prayer up on a roof when the Lord caused him to fall into a trance. God gave Peter a *vision* of a large sheet holding animals that were classified as unclean (**Leviticus 11:4–8**), and commanded Peter to **"kill and eat" verse 13**.

Peter recognized the voice as being God's, but he answered, **"Surely not, Lord!"** When Peter protested this infraction of the Jewish law, the Lord spoke again, saying, **"Do not call anything impure that God has made clean" verse 15.**

5. Peter saw this scene repeated *three* times before the vision was over. Peter was probably reminded of the night he denied Jesus *three* times (**Matthew 26:69–75**). This could have served as a final confirmation for him that what he was hearing really was from God (**verse 16**).

6. Peter was not sure he understood the full meaning of the vision (**verse 17**).

7. The Holy Spirit gave Peter further instruction through a *word of knowledge* in **verses 19–20**. The Holy Spirit knew that the men looking for Peter were Gentiles and that Peter, a devout Jew, would be hesitant to go with them, since visiting the home of a Gentile would make a Jew ceremonially unclean (**verse 28**).

8. As Peter walked in obedience, he received more understanding.

   a. **"But God has shown me that I should not call any man impure or unclean" verse 28.**

b. "I now realize how true it is that God does not show favoritism but accepts men from every nation who fear him and do what is right" verses 34–35.

c. "All the prophets testify about him that everyone who believes in him receives forgiveness of sins through his name" verse 43.

///

As we do what God tells us to do,

we will receive more understanding.

///

9. Cornelius recounts the vision he had. He was in prayer, too, when God gave him the vision (**verses 30–32**).

10. Peter's obedience in preaching the good news about Jesus brought divine results. Even before Peter was finished speaking, the Gentiles were baptized with the Holy Spirit, and they spoke in tongues and praised God (**verses 44–46**).

By allowing the Gentiles to receive the Holy Spirit at this point, the Lord made perfectly clear His acceptance of Gentiles as full-fledged members of His family.

11. It was so important that these Gentiles hear the Gospel that God used supernatural manifestations of the Holy Spirit to get Peter and Cornelius together.

a. God sent an angel to Cornelius and gave him a vision (**verses 3–7**).

b. God gave Peter a vision (**verses 9–16**).

c. God spoke to Peter and gave him explicit instructions (**verses 19–20**).

12. In today's Scriptures, we saw God communicate through visions, dreams, visitations from angels, and the gifts of the Spirit.

    Doesn't it remind you of **Joel 2:28–29**? **"I will pour out my Spirit on all people. Your sons and daughters will prophesy, your old men will dream dreams, your young men will see visions. Even on my servants, both men and women, I will pour out my Spirit in those days."**

    As Christians, shouldn't we be experiencing this today?

13. As we seek God, study His Word and stay yielded to Him, God will choose the manner in which He speaks to each of us. God is able to guide us through the inner knowing, inner voice, authoritative voice, visions or dreams. Our responsibility is to seek God and allow the Holy Spirit to minister through us as He wills.

C. Other Manifestations of the Holy Spirit

1. The manifestations of the Holy Spirit listed in **1 Corinthians 12:7–11**
2. Falling—**John 18:2–6**
3. Dove—**Matthew 3:16**
4. Wind—**Acts 2:2**
5. Fire—**Acts 2:3**
6. Cloud/Glory—**2 Chronicles 5:13–14; Exodus 40:34–35**
7. Fragrance—**2 Corinthians 2:14–15**
8. Angels—**Luke 2:9–11**

ASK IF ANYONE PRESENT HAS EVER SEEN ANY OF THE MANIFESTATIONS WE'VE DISCUSSED TODAY, I.E., DREAMS, VISIONS, FALLING, ANGELS, ETC. ASK FOR A SHOW OF HANDS, BUT DON'T GET INTO A LONG DISCUSSION ABOUT ONE PERSON'S SPECIFIC DREAM OR VISION.

///

The overriding purpose of all the manifestations of the Holy Spirit is to draw people into a saving faith in Jesus, so that they can have a closer relationship with God.

///

IV. Discussion of the Assigned Articles

ASK THE PARTICIPANTS IF THEY HAD A CHANCE TO GO OVER THE SCRIPTURES ON THE ARTICLE **"REVIEW OF HEARING GOD'S VOICE."**

ASK IF ANYONE HAD ANY QUESTIONS OR COMMENTS ABOUT IT.

V. Next Week's Assignment

A. REVIEW NEXT WEEK'S ASSIGNMENT ON THE COURSE OUTLINE.

B. REVIEW THE MAIN PRINCIPLE FOR NEXT WEEK'S LESSON.

C. SUGGEST THAT AS THE CLASS READS **JOHN 20:1–23,** THEY FOCUS THEIR STUDY ON THE THREE PEOPLE IN THIS PASSAGE—MARY MAGDELENE, JOHN AND PETER. ASK THEM

TO LOOK SPECIFICALLY AT WHAT THESE PEOPLES' RESPONSES WERE AS THEY WENT TO THE EMPTY TOMB. HAVE THEM LOOK AT THE GIFTINGS AND STRENGTHS OF EACH ONE AND HOW THEY RELATED TO JESUS IN THIS PASSAGE AND IN OTHER PASSAGES. THIS WILL HELP THEM PREPARE FOR THE DISCUSSION NEXT WEEK. YOU, THE FACILITATOR, WILL LEAD THAT DISCUSSION AS WELL AS A TIME OF BREAKING BREAD TOGETHER.

VI. Ministry Time

A. AS FACILITATOR, YOU NEED TO GUIDE THE MINISTRY TIME. REFER TO THE CLASS FORMAT SECTION OF THE *FACILITATOR TRAINING STUDY GUIDE* AND READ THE "MINISTRY TIME" SECTION. (Note: The *Facilitator Training Study Guide* is the booklet you received during Facilitator Training.)

B. BE SURE TO PRAY FOR THIS WEEK'S DISCUSSION LEADERS. ENCOURAGE PARTICIPANTS TO SHARE ANY SCRIPTURES OR WORDS OF ENCOURAGEMENT THAT THE LORD GAVE FOR THESE LEADERS.

C. NOTE: THE MINISTRY EMPHASIS HAS NOW SHIFTED TO THE WEEKLY DISCUSSION LEADERS. ANY OTHER PERSONAL MINISTRY SHOULD NOW BE ADDRESSED AFTER CLASS UNLESS THE HOLY SPIRIT STRONGLY DIRECTS YOU OTHERWISE.

D. AT THE BEGINNING OF THE MINISTRY TIME YOU MAY WANT TO REMIND PARTICIPANTS:

As we minister to each other, we need to recognize that we are all fine-tuning our hearing of God's voice. We may not hear clearly all the time, so we need to carefully weigh any word of prophecy a class member gives us. The following is a helpful guideline:

If it doesn't make sense, put it on the shelf. If it contradicts what God has told you, let it drop. If your spirit confirms it, make a note of it in your journal and watch God bring it about.

E. ENCOURAGE HANDS-ON MINISTRY BY CLASS MEMBERS. ALLOW THE GIFTS OF THE SPIRIT TO MANIFEST IN DIFFERENT PEOPLE.

F. BE CAREFUL THAT ONE PERSON DOES NOT DOMINATE THE MINISTERING.

G. CLOSE WITH PRAYER.

LESSON 12

"GO TELL!"

MAIN PRINCIPLE

As we remember what Jesus has done for us, we renew our determination to love and follow Him. As we recognize the gift of God within us, we are prepared to go out into the world and bring the good news of reconciliation with God the Father through Jesus by the power of the Holy Spirit.

LESSON 12

"Go Tell!"

I. Let's Get Started!

A. WELCOME THE CLASS AND ENCOURAGE PARTICIPANTS TO SHARE WHAT GOD HAS BEEN DOING IN THEIR LIVES THIS PAST WEEK.

B. OPEN WITH PRAYER.

C. WORSHIP THE LORD.

D. READ, OR HAVE SOMEONE READ, THE MAIN PRINCIPLE FOR TODAY'S LESSON.

THE MATURITY LEVEL OF YOUR CLASS WILL DETERMINE HOW MUCH OF THIS MATERIAL YOU WILL TEACH. IF YOUR GROUP IS ABLE TO DELVE DEEPLY INTO THE SCRIPTURES ON THEIR OWN, YOU WILL BE ABLE TO LEAD A DISCUSSION AS THEY SHARE WHAT GOD GAVE THEM. IF YOUR GROUP IS FAIRLY INEXPERIENCED, YOU WILL NEED TO TEACH MORE OF THE MATERIAL.

THIS LESSON IS QUITE LONG. YOU WILL NEED TO PRAY BEFORE AND DURING CLASS ABOUT WHAT PARTS OF THE MATERIAL YOUR CLASS NEEDS TO COVER. WITH THAT IN MIND, YOU CAN THEN GUIDE THE DISCUSSION TOWARD THE ISSUES IMPORTANT FOR YOUR CLASS.

YOU WILL NEED TO PROVIDE THE MATERIALS
NEEDED TO BREAK BREAD TOGETHER: A CUP,
GRAPE JUICE, A PLATE, BREAD AND A BIBLE.

OFTEN GOD MINISTERS TO CLASS MEMBERS
IN A SPECIAL WAY AT THIS LAST MEETING.
IN PREPARATION FOR CLASS, ASK THE LORD
IF THERE IS ANYTHING HE WOULD HAVE
YOU PRAY FOR OR SAY TO SPECIFIC CLASS
MEMBERS. ALSO, PRAY THAT HE WOULD
GIVE THIS GUIDANCE TO THE ASSISTANT
FACILITATOR AND OTHERS CONCERNING
SPECIFIC CLASS MEMBERS.

II. Supporting Principles From Scripture — John 20:1–23

As we close this 12-week training course, we will look at the
lives of the three people found in this passage. Let's look at
their strengths and gifts, how they related to Jesus, and how
they were obedient in following Him. Look at what these
peoples' responses were as they went to Jesus' empty tomb.

There are other parallel passages in **Matthew**, **Mark** and
Luke which describe this resurrection scene. Because
different people reported what happened, there are some
differences in these stories. We need to patch them together
to get the full picture and use Scripture to interpret Scripture.

A. **"Early on the first day of the week, while it was still
   dark, Mary Magdalene went to the tomb and saw
   that the stone had been removed from the entrance"
   John 20:1.**

1. Mary went to the tomb early while it was still dark.

   a. The Greek word for *dark* is *skotia* (skot-ee´-ah), which has a range of meaning from literal darkness to moral darkness or evil.[1] Mary went to the tomb on the first day of the week. On the first day of creation, God commanded, **"Let there be light"** **Genesis 1:3**. Jesus is the Light of the World, and His resurrection brings us light, life, righteousness and joy.

   b. The Greek word used for *early* is *proi* (pro-ee´). This was a technical term for the last watch of the night—between three o'clock and six o'clock in the morning.[2]

///

Such great love Mary had for Jesus! Her love is woven throughout this passage. **Luke 8:2–3** indicates that this Mary was the woman from whom Jesus had driven out seven demons. She and other women had been with Jesus and His disciples, **"helping to support them out of their own means."** She had served Jesus—ministering to Him and supplying His needs.

///

2. According to **Luke 24:10**, Mary went to the tomb with Joanna, Mary the mother of James, and others.

3. In **Matthew 28:3** an angel of the Lord came, rolled back the stone and sat on it.

   a. What an amazing sight that must have been! **"His appearance was like lightning, and his clothes were white as snow" Matthew 28:3**.

b. In **Matthew 27:62–66** we read that Pilate set a guard at the tomb at the request of the Pharisees. These guards shook from fear of the angel (**Matthew 28:4**).

c. Angels appeared after Jesus was raised from the dead, just as they did at other times in Jesus' life. They appeared to shepherds in Bethlehem to herald His birth (**Luke 2:8–14**). After Jesus' 40-day fast, angels ministered to Him (**Matthew 4:11**). In the Garden of Gethsemane an angel came to Jesus and strengthened him (**Luke 22:43**).

d. In **Matthew 28:5** the angel told the women, **"Do not be afraid."** The Greek word for afraid is *phobeo* (fob-eh´-o), which means "to scare away, to be struck with fear.[3] (It is where we get the English word phobia.)

e. In **Matthew 28:7–8** the angel told the women to **"go quickly and tell his disciples... So the women hurried away from the tomb, afraid yet filled with joy...."**

B. **"So she came running to Simon Peter and the other disciple, the one Jesus loved, and said, 'They have taken the Lord out of the tomb, and we don't know where they have put him!'" John 20:2.**

1. This verse indicates that Mary didn't fully comprehend that Jesus had been resurrected when she went back to tell the disciples.

2. In the parallel passage in **Luke 24:5–11**, Mary and the other women told the 11 disciples and others about what they had seen. They repeated the words of the

angels: **"Why do you look for the living among the dead? He is not here; he has risen!"** However, the disciples did not believe the women **"because their words seemed to them like nonsense."**

3. In **John 20:2** Mary specifically addressed Simon Peter and John. John is the writer of this gospel. He referred to himself in **verse 2** as **"the other disciple, the one Jesus loved."**

4. **A Look at Peter**
   The first person in this passage we want to examine more closely is Peter. In order to understand Peter, it would be helpful to look at what had happened to him before Jesus' resurrection.

   a. **Luke 22:31–34** shows Peter with Jesus at the Last Supper. Jesus said to Simon Peter, **"Simon, Simon, Satan has asked to sift you as wheat. But I have prayed for you, Simon, that your faith may not fail. And when you have turned back, strengthen your brothers"** verses 31–32.

   Jesus said this to Simon Peter in front of all the other disciples. Jesus said "Simon" three times in these verses. This was his old name; Jesus had already renamed him Peter. The name Simon represented his old nature. Jesus knew that Peter's old nature would cause him to deny Him.

How often have we allowed our old natures to dominate us? Perhaps there have been times when we should have stood up for Jesus, declaring that we are Christian. Perhaps we've given in to a habitual sin. We need to realize that Peter, one of Jesus' disciples, had failure in his life, too.

b. In **verse 33** Simon Peter replied, **"Lord, I am ready to go with you to prison and death."** Peter was impetuous and enthusiastic. He was an extrovert, quickly speaking out what he thought.

c. In **verse 34** Jesus answered him, **"I tell you, Peter, before the rooster crows today you will deny three times that you know me."** In this verse Jesus called him Peter, which means *rock*.

///

Fortunately, God doesn't look at our actions as much as He looks at the intent of our hearts. He knew that Simon Peter would fail, but He also knew that Peter would repent and eventually be a strong leader for the other disciples.

///

d. READ **JOHN 18:15–16**. John and Peter followed Jesus after He had been arrested. So, Peter was not alone at this point. John went with him and witnessed what transpired. Perhaps he was there to help Peter because of what Jesus had predicted Peter would do.

e. READ **LUKE 22:54-62**. Peter fulfilled the prophecy of denying Jesus. Can you imagine what it was like for Peter to have Jesus look straight at him after he had denied Him three times (**verse 61**)? This intense fixing of His gaze upon Peter was probably uncomfortable. Yet, Jesus' eyes also expressed His love and forgiveness toward Peter. Peter received that gaze, and went out and wept bitterly (**verse 62**).

///

In spite of our failures, Jesus is quick to forgive us.
He tells us that when we have repented,
we are to go on with what He has called us to do.

///

f. The first words that Jesus said to Peter were, **"Come, follow me" Mark 1:17**, and the last words He spoke to Peter were **"Follow me!" John 21:19**. Peter never failed to follow, even though he stumbled. Jesus knew that even with Peter's faults, Peter would follow Him.

//

A lesson from Peter's life is: It is better to be a follower and fail, than one who fails to follow.

//

C. **"So Peter and the other disciple started for the tomb. Both were running, but the other disciple outran Peter and reached the tomb first. He bent over and looked in at the strips of linen lying there but did not go in" John 20:3–5.**

1. In his excitement to see Jesus, John outran Peter.

2. John stood at the tomb and looked at the linen grave clothes, perhaps reflecting on what may have happened.

D. **"Then Simon Peter, who was behind him, arrived and went into the tomb. He saw the strips of linen lying there, as well as the burial cloth that had been around Jesus' head. The cloth was folded up by itself, separate from the linen" John 20:6–7.**

What they saw has been carefully recorded, so there must be some significance to how the burial linens were found. A burial cloth had been wrapped around Jesus' head and His body had been wrapped by strips of linen. The burial cloth and linens were not found in disarray. The burial cloth from Jesus' head **"was folded up by itself, separate from the linen" verse 7.** Why is this mentioned? Here are some suppositions as to the meaning of these verses:

1. This was to symbolize that Jesus is the head of the church and we are the body of Christ, and that we are separate yet one.

2. The grave clothes were left behind to prove that Jesus' body was not stolen, as some had feared would happen. A robber would not have taken the time to unwrap Jesus or neatly set the linens in place.

3. Jesus left his grave clothes behind to say that death had no dominion over Him (**Romans 6:9**).

4. This could symbolize that when we die to self, we are to put off our old nature (grave clothes) and put on our new nature of righteousness in Christ (**2 Corinthians 5:17; Colossians 3:5–14**).

E. **"Finally the other disciple, who had reached the tomb first, also went inside. He saw and believed. (They still did not understand from Scripture that Jesus had to rise from the dead)" John 20:8–9.**

A look at John, "the other disciple"
The second person we will examine from this passage is John.

1. The fact that John saw and believed says a lot about him. The Greek word for *believed* is *pisteuo* (pist-yoo´-o), which means to put confidence and trust in someone; to have faith; to be persuaded.[5] John had an inner knowing that Jesus had been resurrected.

2. John was tender-hearted and was ready to believe. This was due to the close friendship he had with Christ. John was not more chosen than the rest. He just had a very responsive heart.

3. John saw himself as **"the one whom Jesus loved."** The word *loved* in this phrase has been translated in different verses from both the Greek words *phileo* (fil-eh´-o) and *agapao* (ag-ap-ah´-o). John knew both types of love. *Phileo* is found in **John 20:2**, as we saw earlier, and means to be fond of, have affection for and personal attachment to.[6] *Agapao* is the verb form of the word *agape* and is found in **John 13:23**. *Agapao* means to love ardently, supremely, perfectly.[7] It is how God unconditionally loves the world.

4. God does not love one child of His more than another. Scripture says that God **"shows no partiality" Deuteronomy 10:17; 2 Chronicles 19:7**.

God has no favorites in His kingdom. However, there are some who know how to receive His love more.

5. Apparently, others recognized how close John and Jesus were. In **John 13:21–25** during the Last Supper, Jesus predicted His betrayal. His disciples looked at each other and wondered who it would be. Peter, instead of asking Jesus directly, decided to ask John to inquire of Jesus. Because of the U-shape of the tables commonly used then, Peter could not have been positioned so far from Jesus that he couldn't have asked Jesus himself. Perhaps he thought Jesus might

rebuke him for asking, and felt it was safer to have John ask Jesus.

Sometimes we ask other people to go to the Lord for us. We'll say, "Will you find out from the Lord for me? You seem to have a closer relationship with Him than I do." We might ask this because we are afraid of what God might say to us.

However, there are no favorites in God's kingdom; God wants all His children to be close to Him.

6. In **John 19:25–27** we see more evidence of the close friendship between John and Jesus. When Jesus was hanging in agony on the cross, He looked down at those he loved. **"When Jesus saw his mother there, and the disciple whom he loved standing nearby, he said to his mother, 'Dear woman, here is your son,' and to the disciple, 'Here is your mother.' From that time on, this disciple took her into his home" verses 26–27.**

Scripture indicates that Jesus had other brothers or step-brothers to whom He could have entrusted Mary (**Luke 8:19**). But, Jesus wanted His mother to be cared for by someone who He knew would love her as He did.

//

Because John was able to receive Jesus' love for him,
he was able to love others abundantly.

//

7. Jesus taught all the disciples, yet John seems to have understood at a deeper level.

a. John is the only one who wrote in great detail about the Holy Spirit (**John 14–16**).

b. John's writings offer proof of his deep understanding of love. The word *love* is woven throughout the gospel of **John**. We find it mentioned six times in **chapters 1–12** and 31 times in **chapters 13–17**.

///

A lesson we can learn from John's life is: As we are more and more open to receiving Jesus' love for us, we will be increasingly able to love others.

///

When you know the love of Jesus, it is difficult to withhold it. **"We love because he first loved us" 1 John 4:19.**

F. **"Then the disciples went back to their homes..." John 20:10.**

1. Apparently, Peter did not believe at this point because **Luke 24:12** reads, **"He went away wondering to himself what had happened."**

2. All the disciples had unanswered questions, but Mary was the only one who stayed. What blessings they missed by going home!

Yet we should not judge them too harshly. How many times have we given up because it became too hard? Or, because we didn't know what God was doing and we got discouraged? Have we, during a time of prayer or fasting, given up before a breakthrough or a revelation of God? **"The spirit indeed is willing, but the flesh is weak" Matthew 26:41b (NKJV).**

G. "But Mary stood outside the tomb crying. As she wept, she bent over to look into the tomb and saw two angels in white, seated where Jesus' body had been, one at the head and the other at the foot.

"They asked her, 'Woman, why are you crying?'

"'They have taken my Lord away,' she said, 'and I don't know where they have put him.' At this, she turned around and saw Jesus standing there, but she did not realize that it was Jesus.

"'Woman,' he said, 'why are you crying? Who is it you are looking for?'

"Thinking he was the gardener, she said, 'Sir, if you have carried him away, tell me where you have put him, and I will get him'" John 20:11–15.

A look at Mary Magdalene
Mary is the third person in this passage we will consider more closely.

1. Look at Mary's perseverance! She tenaciously pursued her mission of finding Jesus' body. Mary took this personally. She said, **"They have taken my Lord away ... I don't know where they have put him"** **verse 13.**

   This is even more evident in *The New Testament—An Expanded Translation.* **John 20:15** reads, **"Thinking it was the gardener, [Mary] says to Him, 'Sir, as for you, if you carried Him off, tell me at once where you laid Him, and, as for myself, I will carry Him off.'"** Now this is a mighty woman!

2. Mary's heart was undivided.

    a. Jesus had delivered Mary from seven demons and because of it, she was committed to Jesus. Mary's life is a heart-warming example of gratefulness.

    b. Mary had an obedient, servant's heart and she steadfastly served Jesus and his disciples.

    c. She did not have a complicated faith; it was direct and genuine.

    d. She was more eager to believe and obey than to try to understand everything.

As a result, Mary was honored by being the first person to see the resurrected Jesus face to face. Also, she saw several angels, possibly four, from the different accounts.

H. "Jesus said to her, 'Mary.' She turned toward him and cried out in Aramaic, 'Rabboni!' (which means Teacher)" John 20:16.

    1. Why did Mary not recognize Jesus at first? In **verse 14** it says, **"she turned around and saw Jesus ...."** *Saw* comes from the Greek word *theoreo* (theh-o-reh´-o), meaning to view attentively; to behold something noteworthy.[8] Yet, Mary did not recognize Jesus.

        a. Perhaps it was because she was grief-stricken and crying so much that she couldn't see clearly.

        b. Perhaps it was because she just didn't recognize Him in His resurrected state.

2. However, in **verse 16** when Jesus said to her, **"Mary,"** she recognized Him. Mary responded to Jesus immediately when He called her name.

   a. In **John 10:27** Jesus said, **"My sheep hear my voice, I know them, and they follow me."**

   b. In **Exodus 33:17** we see that the Father knows us by name. **"And the Lord said to Moses, 'I will do the very thing you have asked, because I am pleased with you and I know you by name.'"**

3. It was quite an honor for Mary to see Jesus before anyone else. Her perseverance in seeking Him probably greatly pleased Jesus.

//

A lesson we can learn from Mary's life is:
If we persevere in seeking God, He is pleased and will enable us to know Him better.

//

4. Notice that Jesus relates to women as He created them—as equals and reflectors of God's image.

I. **John 20:17 (AMP)** reads, **"Jesus said to her, 'Do not cling to Me [do not hold Me], for I have not yet ascended to the Father. But *go* to My brethren and *tell* them, I am ascending to My Father and your Father, to My God and your God'"** [emphasis added].

   1. Why not cling to Jesus? Jesus was a touching person, often making contact with people He healed.

      a. In the Jewish religion, the High Priest could not be touched or defiled before he went into the Holy of

Holies, or else he would be struck dead. Perhaps because Jesus was about to go into the Father's presence in heaven, He could not be touched now.

    b. Perhaps He was saying, "Don't try to keep me here. I need to go to the Father and offer my blood to atone for sin."

2. **"Go...tell..."** What a message Mary had to share!

J. **"Mary Magdalene went to the disciples with the news: 'I have seen the Lord!' And she told them that he had said these things to her" John 20:18.**

1. What was their response? In **Mark 16:11** we read, **"When they heard that Jesus was alive and that she had seen him, they did not believe it."**

Have you ever shared something about the supernatural, and people thought you were crazy? Even to the point of trying to convince you that you were crazy?

2. Mary didn't care what they thought!

How important it is for us to trust what the Holy Spirit is saying to us and to walk in the fear of the Lord—not in the fear of man.

K. **"On the evening of that first day of the week, when the disciples were together, with the doors locked for fear of the Jews, Jesus came and stood among them and said, 'Peace be with you!'" John 20:19.**

FACILITATOR:
THE REST OF THIS LESSON SHOULD BE
TAUGHT. WE ENCOURAGE YOU TO REVIEW
THESE SCRIPTURES AND EVENTS SO THAT YOU
CAN TEACH THIS PART FROM YOUR *HEART*.

1. What happened between the time Jesus told Mary to "go tell" and when He appeared to the disciples?

2. First, let's begin by reviewing the events of the last few days.

   a. They ate the Last Supper, during which Jesus endured the heartbreak of knowing His betrayer would be one of His disciples.

   b. Jesus prayed in the Garden of Gethsemane. **"'Father, if you are willing, take this cup from me; yet not my will, but yours be done.' An angel from heaven appeared to him and strengthened him. And being in anguish, he prayed more earnestly, and his sweat was like drops of blood falling to the ground" Luke 22:42–44.**

   c. Judas, His friend, betrayed Him with a kiss. Jesus was unjustly tried, mocked and abused. He didn't say a word because He was so intent on being obedient to His Father. He wanted to redeem God's people so that we could have fellowship with the Father.

   d. Jesus endured the cross—its humiliation and excruciating pain. He forgave the thief, cared for His mother, and was separated from the Father— the greatest pain of all.

e. Jesus died, descended into hell, and was raised from the dead. (**Ephesians 4:9-10**).

3. After His encounter with Mary, Jesus went to the Father as He said He would in **John 20:17**. Like the High Priest in the Old Testament, Jesus went into the Holy of Holies to present His blood as an offering for us, once and for all. READ **HEBREWS 9:11–12**.

4. Think of the rejoicing that went on in heaven! Angels rejoiced when Jesus was born. What would it be like when Jesus returned to heaven as the perfect sacrifice and our High Priest?

5. Jesus returned to walk among His believers to show that He indeed was raised from the dead. He realized the importance of His appearance on earth in His resurrected state. Here was proof of who He was!

6. Jesus entered the room and spoke peace to His disciples to dispel their fear.

L. **"After he said this, he showed them his hands and side. The disciples were overjoyed when they saw the Lord.**
Again Jesus said, 'Peace be with you! As the Father has sent me, I am sending you.' And with that He breathed on them and said, 'Receive the Holy Spirit. If you forgive anyone his sins, they are forgiven; if you do not forgive them, they are not forgiven'" John 20:20–23.

1. Here Jesus is sending them out to preach the Good News, the message of reconciliation between God and man made possible by His sacrifice. The word *send* comes from the Greek word *apostello* (ap-os-tel´-low),

which means to appoint someone, to be sent on a mission, to be commissioned as a messenger.[9]

2. Jesus breathed on them just as God had breathed life into Adam at creation. When Jesus breathed on them and said, **"Receive the Holy Spirit,"** their spirits were filled with God's life (*zoe*) and they were born again. Although they already believed that Jesus was the Messiah, they could not be born again until after Jesus had died, been resurrected, and offered His blood as a living sacrifice for them and for us (**Hebrews 10:10**).

3. During the 40 days He spoke to His disciples and told them to wait until they were clothed with power from God (**Luke 24:49**). This *power* is *dunamis* (doo´-nam-is) in Greek, which is the same power that raised Jesus from the dead (**Philippians 3:10**).[10]

4. Jesus ascended to heaven and asked the Father to send the promised Holy Spirit to be with His followers forever (**John 7:39; John 14:16, 17, 26**).

///

The Lord does not send us out unequipped. We need to be empowered by the Holy Spirit in order to carry out *our* commission from God to preach the Good News and make disciples of Jesus.

///

M. Closing

Let's end with this prayer:
Lord, let our hearts be turned toward Jesus with the perseverance of Mary Magdalene, with willingness to

follow—even if we fail—like Peter, and with the love and compassion of John. May this be all to the glory of our Lord Jesus Christ!

III. Breaking Bread Together

A. A GLASS OF JUICE AND A PLATE OF BREAD MAY BE SET ON A SMALL TABLE IN THE CENTER OF THE ROOM. SAY, "Now as we break bread together, let us remember what Jesus did for us."

B. HAVE THE HOST OR THE ASSISTANT FACILITATOR READ **1 CORINTHIANS 11:23–26**.

C. THEN, EACH BELIEVER MAY PARTAKE OF THE ELEMENTS. THIS CAN BE DONE INDIVIDUALLY OR CORPORATELY, AS THE HOLY SPIRIT LEADS.

IV. Ministry Time

AFTER BREAKING BREAD TOGETHER, BE SENSITIVE TO THE LEADING OF THE HOLY SPIRIT. FOLLOWING ARE SOME SUGGESTIONS TO HELP YOU CLOSE OUT THIS COURSE:

A. THE LORD OFTEN USES THIS TIME TO MINISTER POWERFULLY TO CLASS MEMBERS. ENCOURAGE THE CLASS TO WAIT ON THE LORD SO THAT EACH ONE IS GIVEN DIRECTION OR ENCOURAGEMENT, AS THE LORD DIRECTS. AS FACILITATOR, YOU STILL NEED TO GUIDE THE MINISTRY TIME.

B. THIS COULD BE A TIME TO ENCOURAGE PARTICIPANTS TO SHARE WHAT GOD HAS DONE IN THEIR LIVES DURING THIS COURSE.

C. THE LORD MAY LEAD YOU TO CLOSE WITH A TIME OF WORSHIP AND REJOICING.

V. Ending Note to Facilitators

IF CLASS MEMBERS EXPRESS AN INTEREST IN TAKING ANOTHER ZOE TRAINING COURSE, CONTACT A ZOE REPRESENTATIVE. A LIST OF ZOE COURSE DESCRIPTIONS IS IN THE LESSON 12 SECTION OF THE HEARING GOD'S VOICE STUDY GUIDE.

ENCOURAGE PARTICIPANTS TO READ ABOUT OUR COURSES ON THE WEBSITE AT: WWW.ZOEMINISTRIES.ORG/ZOE-COURSES.

ENDNOTES

Scripture quotations appear from the following versions:

Holy Bible, New International Version, Grand Rapids, Michigan: Zondervan Bible Publishers, 1988.

The Amplified Bible, Grand Rapids, Michigan: Zondervan Publishing House, 1987.

King James Version, Cleveland, Ohio: The World Publishing Co.

New King James Version, Nashville, Tennessee: Thomas Nelson Publishers, 1994.

The New Testament —An Expanded Translation, Kenneth S. Wuest, Iowa Falls, Iowa: Riverside Book and Bible House, 1984.

Life Application Bible-The Living Bible, Wheaton, Illinois: Tyndale House Publishers, Inc. and Youth for Christ USA, 1988.

Scripture quotations are from the *New International Version* **unless otherwise noted.**

Textbook quotations are from *Is That Really You, God?* **by Loren Cunningham. Copyright © 1984, 2001 by Loren Cunningham. Used by permission of YWAM Publishing.**

Lesson 1 - Introduction

1. [disciple] Joseph H. Thayer, D.D., *Thayer's Greek-English Lexicon of the New Testament* (Peabody, Massachusetts: Hendrickson Publishers, Inc., 2000), p. 386, #3101.

2. [full of joy] James Strong, LL.D., S.T.D., *Strong's Exhaustive Concordance of the Bible* (Nashville, Tennessee: Thomas Nelson Publishers), #21.

3. [excerpt from book] Steve Lightle, *Exodus II—Let My People Go* (Kingwood, Texas: Hunter Books, 1983), pp. 33–35.

4. [akouo] Thayer, p. 23, #191.

5. [ginosko] Ibid., p. 117, #1097.

6. [akoloutheo] Ibid., p. 22, #190.

Lesson 2 - Introduction (continued)

1. [spirit, soul, body] Charles R. Solomon, *Handbook to Happiness* (Wheaton, Illinois: Tyndale Publishers, 1989), p. 26.

Lesson 3 - Understanding God's Voice

1. [galah] H.W.F Gesenius, *Gesenius' Hebrew-Chaldee Lexicon to the Old Testament* (Grand Rapids, Michigan: Baker Book House, 1979), # 1540, p. 170.

2. [Jared] Finis Jennings Dake, *Dake's Annotated Reference Bible* (Lawrenceville, Georgia: Dake Bible Sales, Inc., 1963), p. 5, column 4, note b.

3. [Enoch] Ibid., note d.

4. [Enoch-Methuselah] Ibid., note e.

5. [Methuselah] Ibid.

6. [Lamech] Ibid., notes i and n.

7. [Noah] Ibid., note k.

8. [great] Ibid., p. 6, column 1, note s.

9. [grieved] Gesenius, p. 544, #5162.

10. [righteous] Charles Caldwell Ryrie, Th.D., Ph.D., *Ryrie Study Bible—NAS* (Chicago, Illinois: Moody Press, 1978), p. 16, footnote.

11. [the ark] Ibid., note c.

12. [clean/unclean animals] Dake, p. 6, column 2, note t.

13. [God remembered] *The NIV Study Bible* (Grand Rapids, Michigan: Zondervan Publishing House, 1985), p. 16, footnote.

14. [zakar] H.W. F. Gesenius, *Gesenius' Hebrew-Chaldee Lexicon to the Old Testament* (Grand Rapids, Michigan: Baker Book House, 1979), p. 244, #2142.

15. [raven] *The Encyclopedia Americana, Vol. 23* (Danbury, Connecticut: Grolier, Inc., 1993), p. 274.

16. [dove/seeds] *The Encyclopedia Americana, Vol. 9* (1993), p. 316.

Lesson 4 - Spirit, Soul, Body - Whats the Difference

1. [qara] Gesenius, p. 739, #7121.

2. [batsar] Strong, #1219.

3. [pneuma] Ibid., #4151.

4. [pneuma/immortality] Ibid., #4151 within #5590.

5. [psuche] Ibid., #5590 and William Morris, Ed., *The American Heritage Dictionary of the English Language* (Boston, Massachusetts: American Heritage Publishing Co., Inc. and Houghton Mifflin Company, 1969), p. 1181.

6. [psuchikos] *The NIV Study Bible*, p. 1737, footnote 2:14.

7. [sarx] Strong, #4561.

8. [kardia] Allen C. Myers, Ed., *The Eerdmans Bible Dictionary* (Grand Rapids, Michigan: William B. Eerdmans Publishing Company, 1987), p. 471.

Lesson 6 - Obeying the Spirit

1. [devoted] Gesenius, p. 153, #1361.

2. [believe] Strong, #539 and #543.

Lesson 8 - Different Ways God Speaks – Inner Knowing

1. [go ahead] Kenneth Hagin, *How You Can Be Led By The Spirit Of God* (Tulsa, Oklahoma: RHEMA Bible Church AKA Kenneth Hagin Ministries, 1991), p. 25.

2. [uneasiness] Ibid., p. 24.

3. [wait] Ibid., p. 34.

4. [inner knowing] Ibid., p. 27.

5. [open] *Interlinear Greek-English New Testament* (Grand Rapids, Michigan: Baker Book House, 1981), #1272.

6. [compelled by the HS] F.F. Bruce, *The International*

Bible Commentary (Grand Rapids, Michigan: Zondervan Publishing House, 1979), p. 1303.

7. [verse 25] *The NIV Study Bible,* p. 1686.

8. [overseer] Strong, #1985.

Lesson 9 - Different Ways God Speaks – Inner Voice

1. [one accord] Strong, #3661.

2. [dunamis] Ibid., #1411.

3. [grace] Ibid., #5485.

4. [Ananias & Sapphira] Dake, p. 127, column 1, note f.

5. [testing the Spirit] *The NIV Study Bible,* p. 1652, footnote 5:9.

6. [fear of the Lord] Joy Dawson, *Intimate Friendship With God* (Old Tappan, New Jersey: Fleming H. Revel Company, 1986), p. 20.

Lesson 10 - Different Ways God Speaks –Authoritative Voice of the Holy Spirit

1. [graciousness] *New American Standard Bible* (Denver, Colorado: Life For Laymen, 1979), p. 151 footnote.

2. [barrenness] Dake, p. 295, column 1, note k.

3. [peace] Strong, #7965.

4. [favor] Ibid., #2590 and #2603.

5. [remember] *The NIV Study Bible*, p. 16, footnote 8:1.

6. [Samuel] Ibid., 1 Sam. 1:20 textnote c.

7. [until weaned] *The Amplified Bible* (Grand Rapids, Michigan: Zondervan Bible Publishers, 1987), p. 321 footnote.

8. [ephod] *The NIV Study Bible*, p. 378, footnote 2:18.

9. [12 years old] Ibid., p. 379, footnote 3:1.

10. [lampstand] Ibid., foonote 3:3.

11. [know] Gesenius, pp. 333-334, #3045.

12. [words] Dake, p. 298, column 1, note c.

Lesson 11 - Other Manifestations of the Holy Spirit

1. [light] Strong, #5457.

2. [goads] *The Eerdmans Bible Dictionary*, p. 423.

3. [Ananias] *The NIV Study Bible,* p. 1660, footnote 9:10.

4. [grace] Strong, #5485.

5. [word of knowledge] Dick Iverson, *The Holy Spirit Today* (Portland, Oregon: Bible Temple Publishing, 1976), pp. 114–115.

6. [carry] Dake, p. 133, column 1, note l.

7. [apostello] Thayer, p. 67, #649.

8. [Jesus appeared] *The NIV Study Bible*, p. 1660, footnote 9:17.

Lesson 12 - "Go Tell!"

1. [skotia] *The Eerdmans Bible Dictionary*, p. 261.

2. [proi] William Barclay, *Daily Bible Study—Gospel of John, Vol. 2* (Louisville, Kentucky: The Westminster John Know Press and London, England: Hymns Ancient & Modern, 1956), p. 309.

3. [phobeo] Thayer, p. 655, #5399.

4. [phileo] Strong, #5368.

5. [pisteuo] Thayer, pp. 511-512, #4100.

6. [phileo] Strong, #5368.

7. [agapao] Dake, p. 120, col. 1, note m.

8. [thereo] Thayer, p. 290, #2334.

9. [apostello] Thayer, p. 67, #649.

10. [dunamis] Strong, #1411.

APPENDIX

Guidelines for a Personal Visit/Phone Call with Discussion Leaders

1. **Before the visit/call:**

   a. Set up a time to visit/call the couple/class member and tell them what the purpose of the visit/call is.

   b. Ask God what He wants to do in this couple/class member so that you will know how to pray for them personally. Ask for His guidance and protection during your time with the leaders.

   c. Look at the class material so that you will be able to answer any questions they have regarding the book, article and Scripture assignments.

2. **During the visit/call:**

   a. Pray that God would bless your time together and that He would bring to mind those things that need to be discussed.

   b. Ask how they are doing. Ask if they are enjoying the course.

   c. Ask if they have read the article **"Guidelines for Leading a Class Discussion."** Ask if they have any questions about this.

   d. Ask them if they have any questions about the information in the book, article or Scripture assignments. Ask if the Holy Spirit has given them any new insights.

e. Ask if they have questions to stimulate discussion.

f. Encourage them to be open to the Holy Spirit's leading as they prepare and lead the class.

g. Pray together and ask the Lord to anoint them for this task.

3. After the visit/call:

a. Pray for God's anointing, guidance and protection of these participants as they serve as discussion leaders.

b. Pray that God would continue to work in their lives.

www.ingramcontent.com/pod-product-compliance
Lightning Source LLC
Chambersburg PA
CBHW060235050426
42448CB00009B/1449